HOW TO BUILD
Wooden Gates and
Picket Fences

HOW TO BUILD
Wooden Gates and Picket Fences

Second Edition

KEVIN GEIST

STACKPOLE
BOOKS

To Andy—

Life is better with a good partner. Thank you for your support, being the extra set of hands in making and photographing the projects, and editing and giving your honest criticism of this book. You were a tremendous help.

Copyright ©1994, 2011 by Kevin Geist
First edition published 1994. Second edition 2011.

Published by
STACKPOLE BOOKS
5067 Ritter Road
Mechanicsburg, PA 17055
www.stackpolebooks.com

Warning

Although safety precautions are noted throughout this book, they are not meant as substitutes for common sense and caution. All persons following the steps for making the gates and fences in this book do so at their own risk. The author and publisher disclaim any and all liability for any injuries that may result from the execution of the steps provided here.

Printed in the United States of America

10 9 8 7 6 5 4 3 2 1

Cover design by Caroline Stover

Postcard on page 5, courtesy Pequot Library Association; photo on page 6, courtesy Joe Vare; images on pages 45, 47, and 49, courtesy Marilyn Geist; two lower photos on page 62, courtesy Open Sky Media; lower photo on page 65, courtesy Ian Poellet.

Library of Congress Cataloging-in-Publication Data

Geist, Kevin.
    How to build wooden gates and picket fences / Kevin Geist. — 2nd ed.
       p.   cm.
    ISBN-13: 978-0-8117-0766-4 (pbk.)
    ISBN-10: 0-8117-0766-0 (pbk.)
    1. Fences—Design and construction—Amateurs' manuals.   2. Gates—Design and construction—Amateurs' manuals.   I. Title.
TH4965.G45   2011
717—dc22

                                                                    2011007297

Contents

A Beautiful, Functional Fence

Compared with other home construction projects, creating a fence may be less complex than putting on an addition or building a garage, but it does require planning, design, and an understanding of structural concepts. If you want a fence that lasts a lifetime, you need to build it with quality materials and attach it to a sturdy foundation. When maintenance is required you will want to make it easy to replace damaged parts. Yes, you can put a pointed top on a bunch of boards and make a perfectly acceptable, ordinary picket fence, but there are multitudes of beautiful designs to choose from and there is nothing preventing the artist in you from making your own designs.

Fences made society. From the time the first agrarians staked off a piece of land to keep marauding fauna from pillaging the crops, civilization was born. People set physical boundaries on property that defined ownership and limited access.

Top: Forts in early colonial days were not grand stone edifices, but really just palisades, or a large burly version of a picket fence. Above: Early American fences were often crude, simple, and utilitarian structures built to protect gardens, manage livestock, and maintain property division.

1

Visitors to Williamsburg will marvel at the fences displayed in the colonial capital.

Throughout the Colonial Era and early Federal Period of America, fences remained largely practical structures with little ornamental value. Those early Virginia forts were not grand stone edifices, but really just palisades, a large burly version of a picket fence, albeit crude in appearance. Only the wealthy minority had grand and ornate fences around their estates and houses, but most common folks had very crude, simple, and utilitarian fences for the purposes of managing livestock and dividing property.

Managing livestock was the primary purpose for urban fencing. In the days before dairy products were trucked from distant farms, it was necessary for the cows and goats to be close at hand for fresh milk. Even in town, many people owned livestock to supply milk, eggs, and butter for daily meals. Livestock can do a great deal of damage if permitted to wander where they will. In the eighteenth century, Williamsburg had many laws regarding the height, construction, and appearance of fences. It was required of newcomers to construct fences within six months of building their houses.

Today, visitors to Colonial Williamsburg marvel at those fences, yet it would be a mistake to think that the whole of the Virginia colony enjoyed and displayed such charming designs. Finely crafted fences were not for the typical farmer, and few had the money and

status to afford the beautifully cut posts and ornately turned urns and finials that we like to envision when we think of colonial architecture.

From the birth of the nation to the middle of the 1800s, the countryside was dotted with log cabins and only the occasional Georgian, Federal, or Greek Revival mansion. Cruder forms of fencing like split rail and stockade remained common through the middle of the nineteenth century. Then a young landscape architect named Andrew Jackson Downing came upon the stage. He had a vision for transforming the countryside with beautiful Italian-style villas for the wealthy and charming cottages for the less affluent. He was not a big fan of the bulky primitive fences commonly seen in his day. For both homes and fences, he frequently advocated using earth tones to minimize the visual impact of human alterations to the landscape and to blend architecture with its surroundings. Downing's writings laid the groundwork to help establish Italianate and Carpenter Gothic architecture. With those styles came the opportunity for newer, more modern fence designs.

Left: Ornate post urns and finials are often associated with early American fences. Above: Currier and Ives lithographs from the nineteenth century featured the fence as a symbolic part of American home life, as shown here in the print Home on the Mississippi.

Fences were still everywhere in the mid-nineteenth century. Livestock was still taken to market by herding through the streets, and fences in the front yards kept any stray animals off porches and out of gardens. Fences were accepted, even embraced, by the population as part of that American landscape. Currier and Ives lithographs of the period frequently included fences. Their famous "American Homestead" series had a collection of prints depicting each season. The prints showed four different American homes, each one with its own fence.

A contemporary of Downing was architect Samuel Sloan of Philadelphia. He also designed villas for the wealthy and cottages for the common people. Sloan recognized the essential place of fencing in American life. He decided to design fencing that would complement the current architectural modes. While Sloan used wrought- and cast-iron patterns in his works for wealthy clients, he was aware that the cost of those materials was prohibitive for the growing middle class. In the mid-1800s, both lumber and labor were cheap. In his 1852 home designs book, Sloan included patterns for wooden fencing that complemented the cottages that were affordable to the average middle-class citizen. He set a precedent that would be followed by many architects and designers. From that point on, house plan books frequently featured patterns for picket fences and gates.

Sloan's designs, although not as ornate as some to come in the next decade, still required curved exterior and round interior cuts. In 1852, most of these designs would have been cut by hand. It is incredible to think

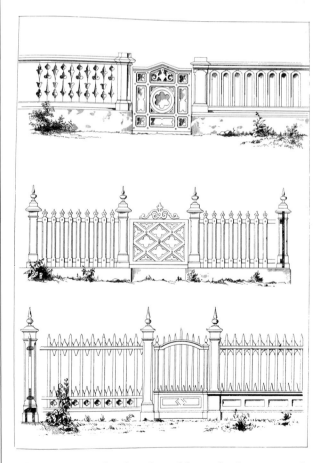

More ornamental styles of wood fences begin to appear in architectural pattern books in the mid 1800s. Samuel Sloan was among the first architects to design decorative fences made from wood and targeted to appeal to the emerging middle class.

of the amount of time and energy that property owners invested in their buildings and structures.

Calvert Vaux, Marcus F. Cummings, and Charles C. Miller followed Sloan with publications for home plans that included decorative fences designed to complement the architecture of their houses. The fence styles were becoming even more ornate, with intricate cuts throughout the bodies of the pickets. Beautifully cut and painted pickets became more and more common, and not just in the garden. Houses themselves were clad with pickets. The fence picket became siding and trim, commonly hung upside down in gable ends and on the edges of the roof eaves.

Further ornamentation came to the fence with decorative layers of wood, or *appliqués*, being used to adorn pickets and other types of grid infill. Inlays also became popular. Previously, it was not uncommon to ornament posts and gates with appliqués and inlays, but individual pickets now began to enjoy this lavish treatment on a more regular basis.

Up until the Civil War, these ornate pickets and fence components were cut using hand tools only, but automated tools were becoming available to make the task easier and faster. The band saw is a tool ideally suited for efficiently cutting curves in wood. The first known band saw design was patented in 1808. Although the mechanics of the saw itself were largely worked out, the science of making strong yet flexible blades for it was not. While America was embroiled in Civil War, blade science was progressing thanks to some persistent French inventors. The band saw became widely used in Europe. By the 1870s, band saws were being used more and more in woodshops throughout America. The new mechanical technology combined with cheap labor and an abundance of lumber lead to easier production.

Wood ornamentation for home and garden structures flourished like never before in history.

Simple and elaborate grid patterns also became more common and some fences became a complex mix of grids, pickets, and panel inserts with intricate carvings and layered appliqués. Gates were often the most lavish part of the fence. After all, a gate is the doorway to the homestead. Making a good impression was important in nineteenth-century society as the middle classes were growing and establishing their status.

No sooner was it possible to create these intricate and multifarious works in wood efficiently when some began to advocate for simpler, cleaner styles. By the end of the nineteenth century, it was uncommon to find newly constructed fences with all this frillery, although posts and gates were often exceptions and continued to be ornamented.

As the twentieth century dawned and the middle class grew, Victorian designs were viewed as too opulent and over-decorated. The Arts and Crafts movement soon rose in popularity. The modern architectural styles of the day favored clean lines. Wooden fences returned to plain styles that matched the simpler lines of the new architectural styles. Picket fences were again being painted white, which they have largely remained to the present.

House plan books still featured fences to match the homes, but ornate curves and curlicues were out in favor of simpler picket, grid, and heavy-duty lattice patterns. Posts could still be ornamented as they were in colonial days, but they were frequently left simple.

The days of virtually every house having a fence was coming to an end. As the twentieth century progressed, one of the primary needs for fencing decreased: there were few animals living in urban areas.

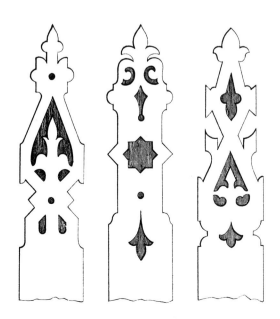

Above: This elaborate ornamental fence was designed by Calvert Vaux in the middle of the nineteenth century. Right: Ornamentation came to the fence with stenciling, carving, cutouts, and layers of wood used to adorn pickets and other types of grid infill.

Left: By the dawn of the twentieth century, most fences had returned to simpler styles, although gate and corner posts often remained ornate. Bottom left: This postcard from the early 1900s features the banker Hugh McLellan's house, built in 1801, complete with ornate fence. Above: Early-twentieth-century bungalows favored basic lines; fences built for them often reflected their clean simplicity.

Most livestock moved out of towns and suburbs into distant rural farms. Modern life made it possible to separate people from the animals they depended upon. Milk and eggs could now be transported with greater ease, making it less essential to have the livestock close at hand. Conversely, even though dogs and cats were not unheard of as pets, in the first half of the twentieth century, the vast majority of households did not have a pet. By the middle of the century, home plan books were more popular than ever, but something was noticeably missing from them. Fence designs were rarely featured.

As the automobile became more common, the need to be close to shopping and work decreased, so suburbs began to sprawl. Many viewed fences as unnecessary in polite society. They were viewed as arcane elements from an outdated past. Huge post–World War II towns and suburbs were created with hundreds of houses, most without a white picket fence.

What seems a bit contradictory is that having a fence was outdated, but the notion of having a fence was not. The phrase "a house with a white picket fence" was, and still is, used to hearken back to the good old days. It expressed the American dream of homeownership, even though new homes usually did not have a fence.

By the 1970s, a change in the American attitude was observed, as a growing pet industry began to emerge in the economy. As the century came to a close, increasing numbers of households included pets. By the dawn of the twenty-first century more than half of the households in the United States had a pet, the most common being a dog. Fences became useful to contain a pet dog outside in the yard and keep it from roaming into the neighbor's property. People began rethinking the other practical uses that fences served. In close communities, fences helped maintain privacy. Even civilized people need to state their boundaries. The key to staying civilized is to state your boundaries nicely.

By the late 1900s, attitudes toward suburban sprawl were shifting, from benign to undesirable. Many saw

By the middle of the twentieth century, the notion of having a house with a picket fence had become a cliché, recalling memories of the good old days. In that era, however, most houses no longer had a picket fence.

The community of Seaside, Florida, founded in 1982, requires each home to have a wood picket fence. Each fence must be of a different style than the others to maintain a level of diversity in the streetscape.

the benefits of being able to work and shop a short distance from the home. New towns and suburbs were formed borrowing from the layout and rules of those earlier close-contact communities. Lot sizes were decreased, amenities were localized, and sometimes picket fences were required to define boundaries while still allowing easy access to talk to the neighbors.

Why a Fence?

Give careful thought to *why* you want a fence. Every aspect of selecting your fence should be a thoughtful process. Everyone who constructs a fence will receive more than one blessing or malediction from it. Forethought and education will maximize your satisfaction and minimize your regrets.

Appearance

A fence can enhance a property's appearance by creating a sense of balance and stability. A house that may appear adrift in a sea of grass is given the appearance of being harbored and secured when contained by a fence. Homes that are close to the sidewalk appear to have more land associated with them when a fence separates them from the street. The fence may complement the structures on the property, possibly by using some of the architectural details in its own design. It harmonizes with the landscaping in some settings, serving as a backdrop for a bed of tulips or a support for climbing clematis or roses.

It enchants the eye with its rhythmic repetitions and symmetrical appearance. Moldings, rosettes, finials, and other detail work on the fence hold the viewer's attention and accentuate the simple repetition.

Boundaries

A fence benefits a property by marking its boundaries. Visually, it can create a sense of definition, showing which areas are inside and which are outside the

property compound. Fence barriers can also be used to separate the property into sections; for example, fenced areas might distinguish the rose garden, the dog run, and the area of the backyard used for the family's recreation.

The fence boundary also helps you control how people pass by your house. A fence can deter passersby from deviating off the sidewalk and cutting across the corner of your yard. The fence openings will help visitors recognize the preferred methods of approach to your home.

Security

Undoubtedly, security was the primary reason the first fences were built. These fences protected the tribe, flock, and crops from predators, both animal and human. Early American pioneers built palisade fortresses that were crude, large-scale picket fences. These fences were a formidable barrier, and their sharp-pointed tops were difficult to climb and straddle.

Through the Colonial, Early American, and Victorian periods, security fencing became more beautiful and more subtle. As rural areas became increasingly urbanized, the cruder branch-and-sapling fences were replaced by elegantly scrolling wrought iron and uniformly sculptured wood picket fencing.

These beautiful fences employed the same pointed tops to discourage climbing; however, the height was reduced and spacing was placed between the pickets, making these fences easier to see over and through. This changed the security formula. Now would-be intruders could see into the yard, but homeowners and neighbors could also see them.

Good fencing was especially useful in town. Fences kept children in the courtyard, away from the dangers of bustling carriages and livestock on the way to market. They were also used to restrain and protect pets.

Almost any fence will increase your property's security. Even a small, easy-to-straddle fence suggests boundary limits. It states that you do not grant access to your property beyond the fence line, letting all intruders know that they are trespassing.

But to protect pets and children or to deter intruders, only certain types of fencing will function appropriately. It is virtually impossible to restrict cats. Most dogs, however, can be contained by a well-designed fence. Fencing to restrain pets must have the appropriate strength, density, and height to prevent the animals from breaking down, squeezing through, or leaping over the fence. Generally, the greater the height of the fence, the greater the security it will provide.

Fencing to protect children has the same density and height requirements as fencing for pets. But since children have the ability to climb, they are able to scale some types of fences, like post and rail, quite easily. Effective fencing for protecting children and securing against intruders must provide no toeholds. Horizontally placed infill, such as post and rail or horizontal spaced board fencing, acts as ladder rungs and facilitates climbing. Vertically placed board, picket, or pale fences are difficult to climb, especially if the pickets are attached to support stringers that are placed wide side to the infill and narrow side up.

Below: Picket fences can be used in the backyard to define boundaries and provide protection for yard and gardens from pets. Above right: Families have long relied on special fences to provide a layer of protection between toddlers and the bustle of the street beyond. Right: This fence does not look imposing, but with its narrowly spaced horizontal boards, it would be difficult to find a place to put your foot to climb over it.

Privacy

Doubtless you have, at least on occasion, had the desire for a privacy fence. We like to view our yards as our personal place where we can get a breath of fresh air, just muddle around, or coddle our loved ones.

Privacy fences can block out unsightly views and limit others' view to your personal outdoor living areas. To achieve a high degree of privacy, the fence must block visibility to the yard. An effective privacy fence is usually 6 feet high with tightly fit infill. Lattice and

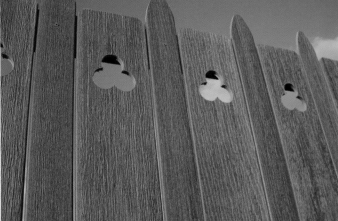

Above: Attractive posts, scalloped fence top, and beautiful plantings make a pretty view and give privacy to the owners. Left: Alternating picket colors and top designs adds interest to a simple privacy fence.

spaced pickets usually make poor privacy fences because they allow moderate visibility through the fence.

Privacy fences have a tendency to be bland in appearance, but you can compensate for this with the following techniques:

- Alternate boards of two or three different widths or heights.
- Decoratively cut board tops with designs that are simple and yet very appealing to the eye.
- Employ two shades of stain or paint to make an appealing contrast.
- Dress the area with shrubbery and flowering plants. The tall fencing will provide a beautiful backdrop.

A privacy fence may affect your property in several ways. It can significantly reduce the amount of sun that reaches the ground, thus limiting the types of plants that will thrive at the base of the fence.

Privacy fences, with their typically high walls, can give the yard a cramped, boxed-in look. This problem is not as noticeable in a large yard, but small yards will appear even smaller when surrounded by a high, solid fence. Additionally, privacy fences have large surfaces that will require up to four times more stain or paint than the average picket fence.

It is not usually necessary to surround your home and yard within a walled fortress. Your fence may be high in the areas where you need more privacy and lower in the areas where privacy is not an issue. Using this approach will allow you to deal with your privacy trouble spots without boxing in your entire yard and blocking out attractive views. If the transition between fence heights is a problem, consider planting trees and shrubs to camouflage that area.

Be well aware that many areas have zoning laws that apply to fence construction. These laws usually require fences to be less than 3 feet, 6 inches on the street side of a property and less than 6 feet high on all other sides of the property. Before constructing any fence, it is a good idea to discuss your plans with your local zoning code officer.

Buffering

For people living near heavily traveled roads, busy factories, or any other noisy, bustling area, noise pollution can cause great distress, especially when one is trying to enjoy an afternoon in the yard. Though a thick, high fence or wall may help buffer the noise, it

Living near a busy road or next to a business with frequent traffic can be a bother. Fences can be used to buffer noise and block headlight beams.

is often difficult to create a fence that will eliminate or significantly reduce the noise level.

Even if a solid fence will not eliminate the noise, it may still reduce your distress. In addition to buffering the noise, it will hide the source of the noise from your view. Often the sight of the noise-causing menace can increase your disdain for the noise itself.

A fence may also serve as a buffer from snow or wind. Snow can present some difficulties. Solid fences generally tend to hold snow. If the fence holds the snow from drifting onto your driveway, this can be desirable. If a significant amount of snow drifts against the fence, however, some sections could topple. Also, fences buried under snow for long periods will decay more rapidly, since prolonged exposure to moisture speeds the decaying process. Spaced fencing will allow the wind to blow the snow through the fence and reduce this problem.

Total wind control is virtually impossible with a fence, although a spaced picket or solid wood fence will supply some wind buffering if it is not located too far from the area to be protected.

Keep in mind when building a fence that a solid fence will allow only very limited sunlight on one or both sides of the fence. This may significantly limit your choice of plants that will grow along the fence.

Choosing a Style

Selecting a fence design is surely the most enjoyable aspect of the planning process. If a primary reason for building a fence is to enhance the beauty of a home, it is important to pay special attention to this step.

Before deciding on a style, create a list of the reasons why you need the fence. As you see styles that appeal to you, you will be able to rate their abilities to meet your needs. When you see a design you like that does not meet all your needs, think of ways you may be able to alter the design.

The style you choose should blend with your house and grounds, complementing the home's overall appearance and function. You may choose your style based on your landscaping and garden. Decorative fences used to accent the landscape are often referred to as "garden fences." A garden fence is attractive to the eye and will offset the greenery and blossoms when they appear. The fence can become the common thread that pulls all your plantings together.

Pattern

Pattern is the most obvious way to choose a fence design to match your house and property. Look for a pattern that is already present on your house and use that pattern in your fence design.

If you're lucky, there may be a picket pattern hanging on the side of your house already. Some houses have accent siding hung vertically beneath the gables. Look at the trim for inspiration. Examine the rooftop and edges. You may see your design there. Windows, doors, porches, and bays are all good places to look when collecting ideas for a potential fence design. Some houses have abundant patterns used on their exterior that are suitable for repeating in your fence. If you don't see obvious patterns, consider some of these

Picket fences lend charm and beauty to your garden throughout the year, especially as flowers begin to bloom.

Left: Here the fence repeats the pattern of the newel post and banister on the porch. Below: This beach-town bar and grill wants passersby to know it's a great watering hole.

A peach-colored picket fence with cream accents matches the colors used on the porch and trim of this Cape Cod–style house.

more subtle, but often equally appealing ways to match your fence to your home.

If you don't have a distinctive pattern on your house, consider color.

Color

Although the popular cliché has preserved the "house with a white picket fence" as an ideal, fences do not have to be white. Colors used on the home's exterior can be repeated on the fence and used to make even a simple design appear more elaborate and intricate. Often people will be fooled into remembering the fence as more ornate than it really is. Many homes feature one, two, or three trim colors in addition to the primary color of the home. If the fence already has an elaborate pattern, highlighting it with just the right colors can make for a breathtaking streetscape that ties the home and fence together.

But when it comes to color, you need not be limited to matching structures on the property. Natural colors and earth tones complement the surrounding landscape and make beautiful fences that harmonize with the grays, greens, and browns of nature. As romantic as the old phrase about the white fence may sound, the sight of a reasonably well maintained yet slightly weathered, natural-toned, fence has its own comfortable charm.

Finally, after all this, let me say you may still want to consider white for your fence. There are reasons why the white fence has earned a place in so many people's hearts. White gives the appearance of crispness and cleanness and serves as a bold backdrop for the greens and other colors of summer lawns and gardens. But still, white is not very distinctive when it comes to fences and a white fence will not create a visual tie to a white house the way a yellow fence would to a yellow house.

Top: The vivid colors of these simple pickets make them pop while linking the fence's color scheme to the house. Center: Earth tones of taupe, tan, beige, and brown can provide relief from the typical white picket fence and allow your garden and landscape to stand out against their muted shades. Bottom: This fence reflects the house colors of white, yellow, and pale blue. The yellow posts complement the variegated yellow and green foliage of the shrub row, while the traditional white pickets act as their backdrop.

Line

One of the most revealing aspects of a home is line. The lines of the house are visible from a greater distance than the finer trim details. The broader curves and angles of roofs, dormers, chimneys, porches, bays, and overhangs all add interest to a house. What is more, you can use those lines to tie your fence into your home.

The pitch of the roof is often prominently noticeable from the street below. Using your roofline angle in the design of your fence is one way to tie your fence design to that of your home. But how? A simple way to is to cut the angle of your picket tops to match the angle of your roof. If the pitch of your roof elevates at 45 degrees, individual pickets cut to the same angle as your roof will complement your home's roofline. If your roof has a distinctive color that is visible from below, the picket tops could also be colored to match your roof.

Making grid and lattice panel designs that mimic the house's roofline is another option for creating a complementary look. Again, find or create a pattern using that same angle of the roof.

In addition to the roofline, look to the most distinctive or pronounced aspects of your house and consider using the lines in your fence. Often porches feature columns with a slight taper or overhangs with a distinctive curve. Repeating these curves and angles will tie everything together in an eye-pleasing way. Most passersby will admire it, but not be able to put their fingers on just why the fence looks so good.

Left: A simple way to mimic lines and angles from your house is to cut the angle of your picket tops to match the angle of your rooflines. Below: This computer-simulated fence design borrows the strong vertical lines of the porch banister for its lower section and the distinct angles of the roofline for the upper section.

Weight

When you think about your house's outside impression, what words come to mind? Delicate or bold? Massive or diminutive? Cozy or roomy? Expansive or condensed? If you find that you have consistently chosen words denoting smaller sizes, you will want a fence to complement that smaller size and not overpower the house. If you have picked all the larger words to describe your house, you will want a fence with some heft, avoiding designs that are too petite. A good awareness of the weight of your house and property structures will help you choose an appropriate fence style.

What if your house is a bit of a contradiction? You might have a cozy little bungalow with massive columns on the front porch and an imposing set of pilasters by the front door. You could get away with doing either a refined or massive fence; either weight would seem acceptable in this case. But, you could have the fence design reinforce the mix in the house, possibly choosing slender pales for your infill with massive posts at the corners and the gate openings.

Left: The fence here is very simple and the porch on the house is very ornate, but this looks like a good match. Why? In addition to the color match, the pickets have adequate depth thickness and the fence posts are a perfect visual weight match to the porch posts. Below: A delicate fence with small 4 x 4 posts would be too understated for this property. This mansion calls for a substantial-looking fence.

Infill, Post, and Gate Considerations

When people refer to a fence, they may be talking about the *infill*, the posts and the gates collectively. Often they are speaking specifically about what makes up most of the surface of your fence. The infill is the skin or fabric of your fence. It is the stationary part that hangs between the posts. In most cases, one section of infill will be made of many pieces of lumber. There are two levels of complexity to the infill: the making of the individual pieces and the task of putting the pieces together and mounting them between the posts.

Making more complicated pieces will increase the amount of time that it takes to cut those pieces. Increasing the number of different types of pieces to make a section of infill increases the complexity of assembling the infill. It is every fence builder's goal to have a fence that is interesting to the eye without being too tedious and difficult to construct.

Top right: This lavish post is adorned with raised panels, chamfered edges, molded caps and bases, and an ornate finial. A common 4 x 4 is at its core, with decorative molding attached over top to create the illusion of a much larger post. Right: Massive posts cut from solid timber have a tendency to crack as the lumber dries. That is why most large decorative posts are built-up with thinner lumber that is less likely to crack as it ages. Below and below right: This may look like a massive solid post at first glance, but with the post cap removed, you can see that it has a smaller core post clad in thinner 2x lumber.

Post Decoration

Posts can range in decoration from a simple bevel-cut top to lavish posts, adorned with raised panels, chamfered edges, molded caps and bases, and ornate finials.

Ornate posts can be created by attaching moldings to solid 4 x 4, 5 x 5, or 6 x 6 posts. A common drawback to using solid-wood decorative posts is that many will crack and split as they age. The thicker a piece of lumber, the greater the chance it will crack through time. It is much more common for thick posts to crack than it is for thinner boards. Also, larger-sized posts, like 6 x 6 posts, are heavier, making them more difficult to handle, and require larger holes to be dug to set them. These can be unnecessary burdens if a larger-sized post is not required.

To avoid the problems associated with larger posts, many people partially encase their decorative posts. With an encased post, there is a smaller core post that has its aboveground portion encased in lumber to make it appear larger. The encasement lumber is usually of a higher quality and less likely to crack than the core post. This method reduces the post's weight and lumber cost while minimizing the chances of splitting and cracking.

If you decide to use ornate posts, space them evenly along the length of the fence. If the spacing is not even, the decorated post will draw attention to the irregularity and detract from the fence's beauty rather than adding to it. An alternative to having every post decorated is to place ornate posts just at gates or corners and leave all the intermediate posts simple. If your intermediate posts are unevenly spaced, this helps draw attention away from the simple posts and toward the ornate posts. Another plus to this approach is that you have very few posts to decorate, while still giving your fence lovely accent pieces.

Gate Design

Gate openings must provide adequate passage for people. Small gates are usually at least 3 feet wide. Gates wider than 5 feet need extra support or should be divided into double-door gates. A double-door gate has one door that is opened frequently and one that remains stationary and is opened only when large items must pass through. Cane bolts, sold at hardware stores, can be used to hold the stationary side of the gate in place.

This double-door gate has one door that is opened frequently and one that remains stationary and is opened only when large items must pass through. A cane bolt goes down into the walkway to keep the stationary side secured.

There are not many rules about choosing a style of gate for your fence. Gates can be designed to blend in with, contrast with, or accent the fence.

Hidden Gates

The overall fence pattern is incorporated into the hidden gate. Sometimes this is done for security reasons: The gate opening is camouflaged and difficult to identify. Others are designed in this fashion to continue the flow of the fence rhythm, enhancing its aesthetic beauty. This approach is also useful in situations where unevenly sized or spaced gates are necessary for functional reasons.

Contrasting Gates

A contrasting gate can beautify a fence while serving a functional purpose: It leads visitors to the entrance by drawing attention to itself. But you do not want a contrasting gate that conflicts with your fence. Experiment by making a scale drawing of the gate with the

fence. Or if you would like to reuse an existing gate, try standing it next to the fence. If the combination is appealing to you, hang the gate; if not, design a more complementary gate.

Accenting Gates

Accenting gates borrow features from the fence's overall design yet contain details that make the gate stand out from the fence. These gates have a special beauty because they combine elements that are both similar and dissimilar to the overall fence, showing the designer's ability to artfully blend the components to produce a masterful centerpiece. Accenting gates borrow a significant benefit from each of the other gate styles. Like contrasting gates, they draw attention to themselves, allowing visitors to easily find the acceptable entrances, but like hidden gates, they incorporate details from the fence in their design and form a unifying link between two separate sections of the fence.

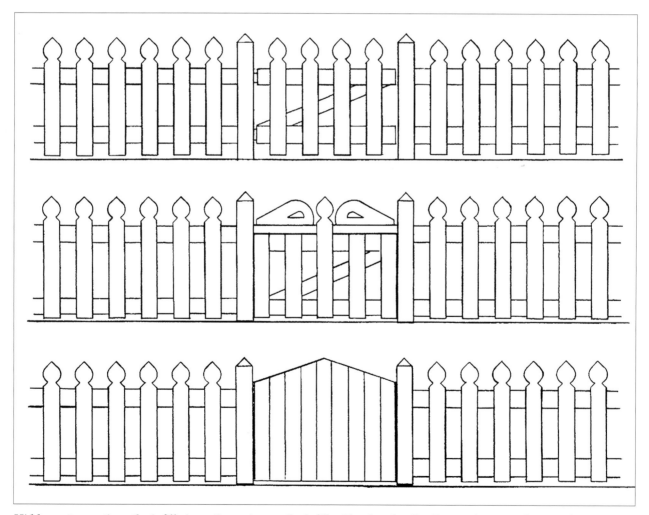

Hidden gates continue the infill. Accenting gates use the infill with other details. Contrasting gates have nothing in common with the infill. But all three types can look great with a fence.

Rather than having a gate at the sidewalk, this fence wraps around to the front door walkway, allowing the residents to enter the house without needing to open both a gate and a door. The gate to the yard is neatly concealed on the path to the door.

No Gate

Gates do slow you down on the way to your house. Yet without a gate, your fence will not provide the protection and security needed to keep small children and pets contained. But maybe you do not have small children or pets, so a gate may not be a requirement of your fence. Sometimes it may be possible to place your fencing right up to your front door and eliminate the need for a gate between your sidewalk and your house.

Siting the Fence and Gates

Exactly where on the property do you want to place the fence? Can you put it on the property line with your neighbor? How high should you make it? Can you use any material you want? How many gates will you need? How wide should the gates be? Who decides the answers to these questions? In this chapter we'll address what requirements you must fulfill before beginning construction.

Getting Permission to Build

Homeowners associations, historical review boards, architectural review boards, zoning boards, and municipal building codes and the officers who enforce them may have an influence on the final fence you erect.

Generally speaking, associations and review boards will be more concerned with acceptable appearance, zoning boards with the impact to the rest of the community, and building codes officers with the safety and functionality of the fence. But all these groups with their rules, codes, and laws are aimed to make sure that you and everyone else living in the area create good-looking, sturdy structures that promote positive reactions from the community.

In many ways the requirements of these groups can overlap. These groups frequently have a joint approval process for residents to use when constructing a fence. You should contact your municipal government office or homeowners association to find out if you will need a permit to put up your fence and what procedures you will need to go through in order to get that permit. Different localities have different requirements that you must adhere to in your project.

People are often put off by the thought that other people should have a say in their fence. If you need to submit an application for this project, the burden is on you to show that your fence will do no harm. You have a better chance of selling your fence to these groups if you can show that it will be beautiful, properly located, and well constructed.

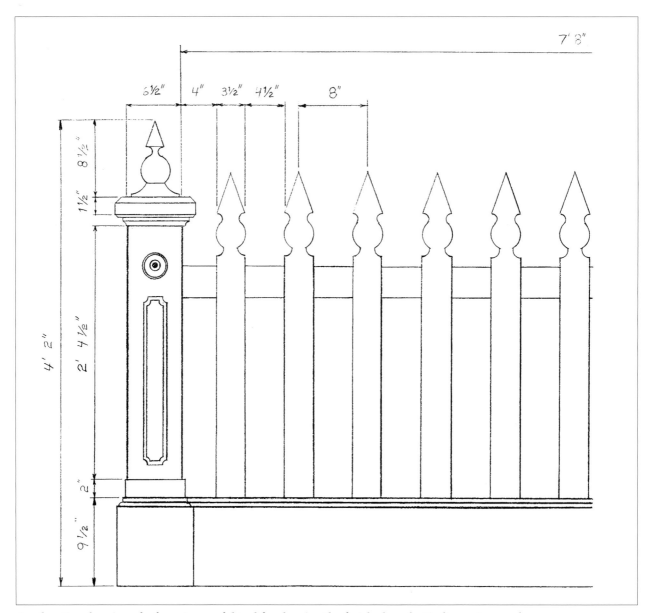

An elevation drawing of a fence is a useful tool for showing the finished product's dimensions and appearance.

Assessing the Project

If you have never built a fence before, you will want to assess the project to determine whether you have what it takes to complete it. We will examine the four Ts—tools, talent, time, and treasure—for you to get a better handle on the project.

■ **Tools.** Do you own the tools you need? Should you buy, borrow, or rent them?

If you have many postholes to dig, you may want to rent or borrow a gas-powered posthole auger, or you may want to hire the job out to a contractor. On the other hand, a hammer and a cordless drill are useful tools that every homeowner should have in their tool chest. For a list of typical tools needed, see page 34.

■ **Talent.** Do you know how to use the tools? Are you willing to learn? Many high schools, vocational-technical schools, and community colleges offer beginner and intermediate adult woodworking classes. They can be great refreshers if it has been years since you have taken woodshop in high school. If you have never taken a woodshop class or it has been quite a while since you have done work in a woodshop, I highly recommend a course with an experienced teacher. You do not need to be a master craftsman. Picket fences are not fine cabinetry and do not require a high degree of precision workmanship. Yes, you will want to make gates that function properly, but when cutting pickets, you need not be concerned that they match perfectly. Minor differences between pickets will show that your fence is handmade, as opposed to factory cast.

■ **Time.** Do you have the time to spend on this project? Do you *want* to invest time on every part of the project? You may enjoy some aspects of fence building but not others. I find digging postholes to be hard and boring work; however, I have always enjoyed cutting pickets. You may want to do it all, but you may prefer having someone else do parts of the job. I myself would rather cut the pickets, assemble the fence, and set the posts in holes that someone else dug for me.

■ **Treasure.** How much money are you willing and able to spend on your fence? Your budget will help determine your limits and flexibility for your project. You may want to have a contractor do certain phases while you reserve others for yourself to do. Of course, the more you have a contractor do, the more it will cost. Often the expense for the needed power tools and materials is well below the cost of hiring out the job, and the tools will then be yours for your future use. You will be able to calculate the materials cost when you have determined the fence's design, the perimeter, and the lumber species or type you want to use. Knowing the perimeter of your fence will tell you how many posts and sections of infill you will need. This will be necessary to identify the total quantity of lumber. Knowing the material you want to use will allow you to contact a lumberyard, mill, or other dealer to get individual lumber prices by dimension. Fasteners, hinges, latches, and gates will also need to be counted and estimated.

Some local governments have their rules online. Many of the items they require will be a benefit to you in seeing your fence to completion. The following items may be required:

- A property diagram showing the perimeter of your fence

- A completed application form for a permit giving specific details of your fence

- Requirements for fence and post height for front yards, side yards, and backyards

- Minimum and maximum requirements on fence opacity, or how far apart the infill must be spaced

- Requirements on post footings and spacing

- Lists of acceptable fence materials and styles

- Proof that the fence is in harmony with the architectural style of the neighborhood streetscape

- Utilities contacted to mark underground wire or pipe locations

- Good-neighbor rules pertaining to the surrounding properties

- Abutting property owners notified

- Best side of fence faces out

- Fencing does not restrict the view from neighboring residents' properties

Planning the Location

An assist to planning the fence perimeter will be an aerial view, or plan view, of your property. The plan view should show existing buildings and structures, such as the house, garage, sheds, patios, decks, gazebos, walkways, and any other permanent structures, as well as significant trees and shrubs. All these items will affect where you can place your fence. You may elect to remove or alter some of them to accommodate the fence.

Once you have a complete physical aerial view of your property, you should next identify the paths of all your traffic routes and areas of activity. Visual inspection of these paths will help you determine where you want to put the fence and where you need gates.

Locating the Posts

Next you need to determine the number of posts you will require. In general, you will need posts at every corner your fence will turn and additional posts flanking each gate. Your posts must be able to adequately support the gate's infill. Post sizes and spacing can vary greatly depending on the density, thickness, and height of the infill. The space between your posts must not be too great, or stringers will easily sway when pressed against.

Post spacing is also important for aesthetic reasons. Posts spaced at even distances add visual appeal to the fence because of their rhythmic high points, while unevenly spaced posts will detract from a fence's appearance.

Unfortunately, if you have a number of gates along the same fence wall, you may be forced to have posts unevenly spaced. If this is the case, you do not want to make ornate intermediate posts; highly decorated posts will draw attention to themselves and make the uneven spacing more obvious. Choose simple posts or hide your posts behind the infill. If your fence will need to be attractive from both sides, or if your design requires integrated posts, try using double posts.

Double posts placed at gates, corners, or gates and corners can be used to take up the slack when numerous gates or odd fence stretches require uneven post placement. Draw your post placement on paper to help you visualize the best locations for your double posts.

Fence posts can be placed in front of or behind the fence infill, or with infill in between the posts. Here are some guidelines to help you determine the best choices for you.

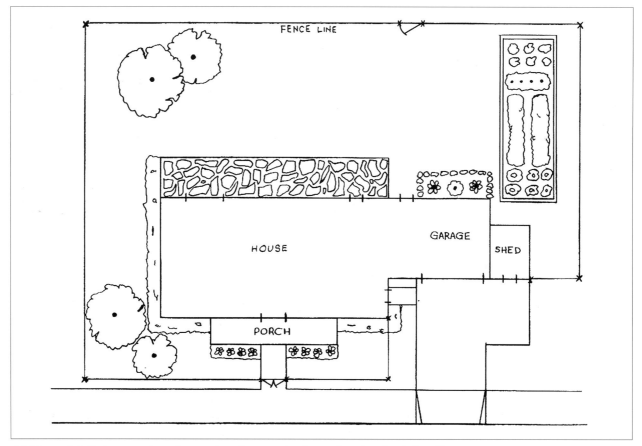

Add fence details to your plan view, such as fence perimeter and post and gate locations.

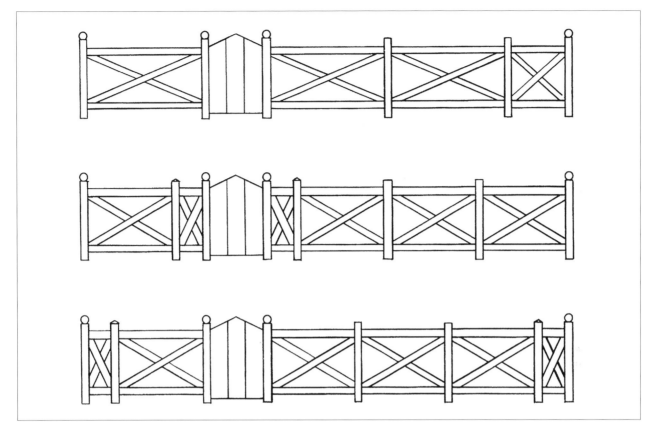

Double posts placed at gates, corners, or both can be used to take up the slack when numerous gates or odd fence stretches require uneven post placement.

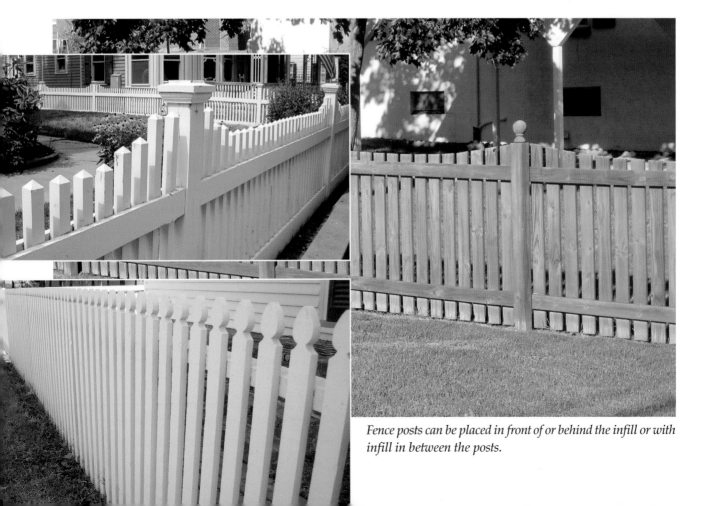

Fence posts can be placed in front of or behind the infill or with infill in between the posts.

Don't skimp on gate locations. Put them wherever you need them. It will be more work to add a gate after the fence is completed.

Placing posts behind the fence is usually the fastest, easiest way to make an attractive fence. This method allows for stringers to be placed either between or in front of the posts. When the infill is attached, it partially or fully conceals the posts from view. This is helpful if post spacing is uneven. The uneven posts, however, will still be visible from the back side of the fence.

Fences in which the infill runs between the posts will reveal the entire post. If the post spacing is even, this is usually the most attractive choice. The rhythmic break in the fence pattern will catch the eye and enchant passersby.

Placing posts in front of the infill is a third alternative. This is the least common way of making a fence. Here, what would normally be considered the back side of the fence is the front. Displaying the stringers in front of the infill can be especially charming, however, if the stringers have a molded edge.

Locating the Gates

Where do I put them? How many will I need? How wide should they be? Should they all look exactly the same? Will single- or double-door gates work better for me? These are a few of the questions all gate builders should ask themselves before starting construction.

The primary reason for a gate is to allow passage into or outside a fenced area. While this statement may seem obvious, many fence builders do not give enough serious thought to the present and future traffic patterns of the residence.

Gates should be strategically placed, sized, and constructed to allow easy, unhindered traffic to and from the residence. Even if you use only the front door now, consider the possibility that one day you may use the side door as well, and you may want a gate close to that door too. It is much easier to design several gates into the fence from the start than to add one or two after posts have been set or the fence completed.

Tools and Materials

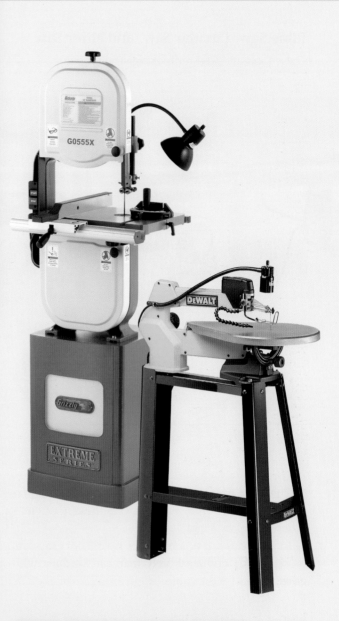

In this chapter I will discuss some of the most common tools used in fence construction. The basics of fence construction can be understood and applied by just about anyone. There is little variation in structural frames for fences. Creating infill is usually a matter of cutting repetitive pieces. Hanging gates requires patience and care but is not technically difficult. Confidence, desire, and a good assistant for certain phases of the project will provide the amateur carpenter with all the support needed to complete the fence.

Tools for Doing It Yourself

If you decide to build the fence yourself, you will want to be able to safely and effectively operate some power tools. Before using any piece of machinery you buy or borrow, you should always read and understand the owner's manual. Heed all safety recommendations, such as wearing eye protection and removing all loose-fitting clothing and jewelry.

Many tools have guards and guides designed to expose only the minimum amount of the blade needed to make the cuts. In the photographs, for the sake of illustrating the cuts, the blade guards have been removed and guides lifted higher than is necessary. These guards and guides do reduce incidents of injury and in many cases help you do a better job of cutting and holding your lumber. Adjust yours so that you expose only the amount of the blade you need to cut your workpiece and no more.

Table Saw, Circular Saw, and Miter Saw

These tools are used for making straight cuts.

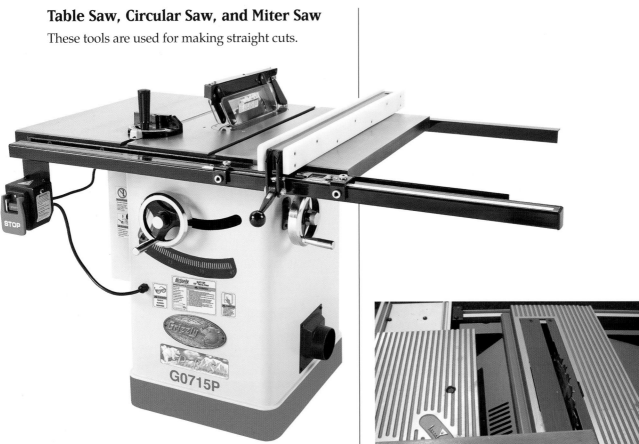

The **table saw** has a round blade, like the circular saw, but rather than being a handheld tool, it is mounted below a table.

In most cases, it accomplishes rip cuts or crosscuts more quickly and accurately than can be done with other saws.

Crosscuts are made across the grain of the wood and are made using a sliding miter guide or crosscut sled to pass the workpiece through the blade.

Rip cuts are made following the grain of the wood. The table saw's rip fence helps the user guide the workpiece through the blade.

Table saws usually have a safety device called a *blade guard*, which is designed to expose the minimum amount of blade needed to make the cut. The guard will rise to the height of the lumber as you feed it through the blade.

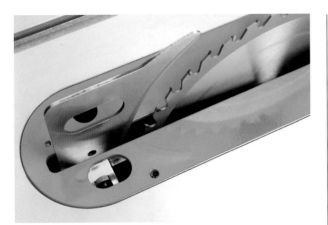

The *splitter* (above) is another safety device that sits behind the blade. Without it, the lumber can close or bind on the spinning blade, throwing the wood back at you with great force.

Table saws allow you to raise and lower the blade to different heights. They also enable you to change the angle of the blade and the angle of the miter guide. Changing the angle on both the blade and the miter guide will allow you to cut compound angles. These abilities can be very useful for creating post, gate, and infill components. If you have access to a table saw with a *tenoning jig* (below), which is used to securely hold small or narrow pieces of lumber, you will be able to make beautiful raised panel appliqués and beveled post caps.

The **circular saw** is a handheld power tool that is most useful at the fence setup site. It comes in corded form for constant cutting ability and cordless varieties that allow you to cut even where there is no power source. The circular saw also has the ability to do both rip cuts and crosscuts, making it a versatile tool at the job site. Since a large area of the circular saw's blade can be exposed, it has the potential to be one of the more dangerous power tools. Always operate a circular saw with extreme care.

The circular saw has much practical use in cutting stringers, posts, and other members to length. It also has the ability to cut angles by adjusting the plate to the specified degree between 0 and 45. This ability allows you to cut mitered post tops. It also allows users to create decorative chamfers in lumber.

tenoning jig

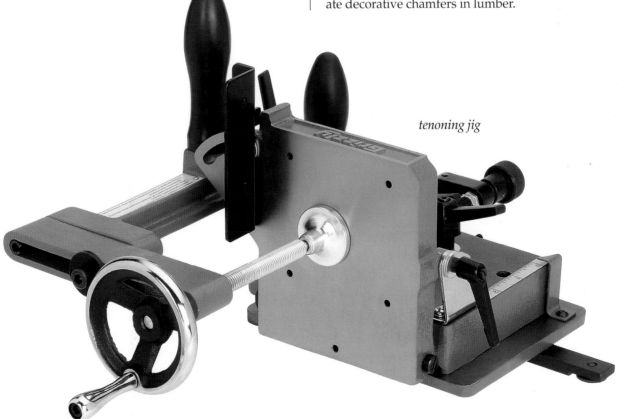

You can also make straight cuts with the **miter saw**. It is fine for doing crosscuts and super at cutting angles and compound angles, but you cannot do rip cuts on a miter saw. If you don't need to do rip cuts, the miter saw can substitute for a table saw.

Band Saw, Jigsaw, and Scroll Saw

With these tools you can make a variety of curved cuts as well as straight cuts.

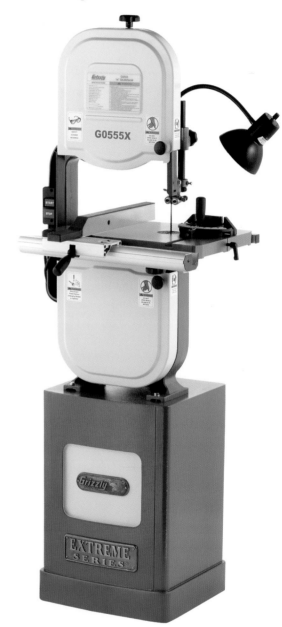

Band saws are ideal for making short, straight cuts. When I make small notches and blind stops, I use my band saw. It provides greater precision than a table saw can. But the big advantage of a band saw is its ability to cut curves.

The band saw cuts curves that would be impossible to make with the wide, flat blade of the circular saw. The band saw's blade is a continuous band of metal that runs on two or three wheels. Three-wheel models tend to be small and bench-top saws are usually best suited to craft projects in which you are working with small pieces of thin wood. Most three-wheel bandsaws are too small to effectively cut pickets of 1x or thicker material.

For all the projects in this book, you will need a band saw that allows you to cut wood that is up to 6 inches thick. You do not need a large band saw for these projects. I used this 14-inch model, which is among the smallest of floor-model band saws, to do all the projects in this book.

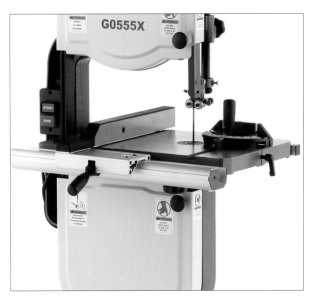

Band saws also can have miter guides and rip fences, which are used to make straight cuts at various angles similar to the table saw.

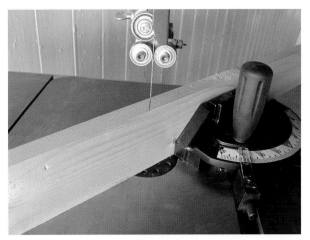

Most medium and large band saws will have only two wheels, with one wheel located above the cutting table and the other below it. All the cutting a band saw does occurs on its table in the space between the wheels.

Band saw blades are thinner than table saw blades, so they tend to create less dust and less wood waste. Generally speaking, the smaller the blade, the better it is for cutting tight curves; the wider the blade, the better it is for cutting straight. Unlike the table saw, the band saw pulls the wood down onto the table, preventing the blade from throwing the wood back at you.

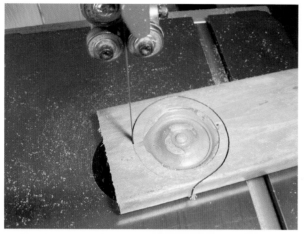

The flexible properties of the band saw allow you to make a variety of scrolling cuts that are very useful in creating decorative pickets, post tops, and gate scrolls. If your picket has many curved cuts and a few straight cuts, you need not switch machines; you can do the straight cuts on the band saw too. The band saw can make beautiful fretwork even in thick lumber such as 2x and 4x material.

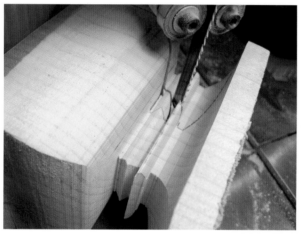

The band saw will also allow you to make magnificent finials to adorn your posts and in a fraction of the time it would take to make turned finials on a lathe.

Although the band saw can do a host of amazing things, there is one thing it cannot do. Its continuous loop blade does not allow you to make cuts on the interior of a board. For that you need a jigsaw or a fretsaw.

Jigsaws are handheld saws that allow you to make scrolling cuts. To make interior cuts with a jigsaw you must first drill a hole in the lumber before you start cutting, so that you can insert the blade through the hole.

Jigsaws are frequently used to scallop the tops of fences after the pickets have been installed.

Router

The router is another useful tool for making decorative moldings and fretwork for your fence. Routers can be used to make fine detailed moldings on baseboards, raised panels to incorporate in the infill or on posts, and decorative post tops. When using thin lumber, the router can cut out scrolling patterns, using a template, with greater accuracy and speed than the band saw, jigsaw, or fretsaw. The only caveat is to watch the thickness of the wood; most fence lumber tends to be thicker than can be efficiently cut using a router.

Fretsaws, which also require a hole be drilled in the wood before you make interior cuts, have a table and arms to hold a blade that you insert in the hole and then fasten to both arms. The straight blades of both the jigsaw and the fretsaw move up and down to cut the work. This back-and-forth movement creates some degree of vibration, making the fretsaws less pleasant and much slower at cutting than band saws. For those reasons, I recommend that you try to use the band saw for all of your curved cuts. For true interior cuts, however, you will need to bite the bullet and use the fretsaw or jigsaw.

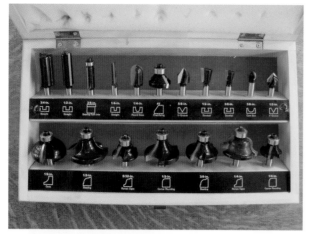

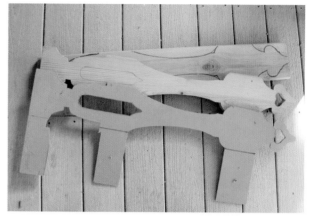

To make decorative moldings, such as that on top of a baseboard, you use a decorative cutting bit with a bearing guide. There are a variety of router bits for making different profiles in your lumber. Bits with a bearing guide, like the entire bottom row in the bit set above, are used to make decorative edges. Bits with no bearing guide, like most of those in the top row, can be used to make detailed veins and rosettes. To make those veins perfectly straight and rosettes perfectly round, you will probably need to use some accessories.

You can purchase router bits made of all high-speed steel or ones that are carbide-tipped. Carbide-tipped router bits are more expensive than other kinds, but they will last much longer and produce better output.

Special pattern bits are available for cutting out patterns with a router. To make scrollwork with a router, you need a wood template. Cardboard templates do not give the router bit's guide bearing the firm surface it requires for a clean cut. Trace the pattern onto a piece of pressed hardboard and cut it out using a band saw. Strict attention to the cutting line is imperative; this is the template from which every picket or scroll bracket will be made. Templates should be nailed or screwed to the workpiece. With the router mounted on a router table, the workpiece is fed into the router bit until the guide bearing and template contact. The guide bearing of the pattern bit will ride along the template edge while cutting through the workpiece.

Router bits are mounted below the router. This ogee profile bit is frequently used to rout decorative edges on baseboards.

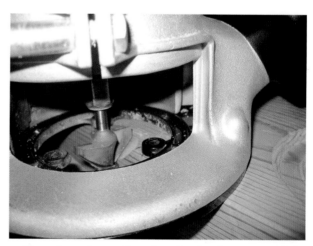

To make a decorative chamfer for the corner of the post casing, a 45-degree angle bit with bearing guide is used. The workpiece is fed through the router while the template is kept against the pattern bit's guide bearing. After going all the way around the template, the picket or scroll bracket is completely cut out. The template can also be clamped to the workpiece on a workbench. The handheld router can then be traced around the edge of the template to cut out the design.

I have routed individual picket edges and designs on pickets using a router and template. While it looks great, it does take more time to do that extra step, and it is only visible up close.

While the router is not a required tool for making a fence, it can help you make your fence interesting. There are many router accessories that allow you to add detailing in your lumber like chamfers, veins, and rosettes.

A parallel guide attachment for your router will allow it to ride along the edge of the lumber and make straight veins of the interior surface of the lumber.

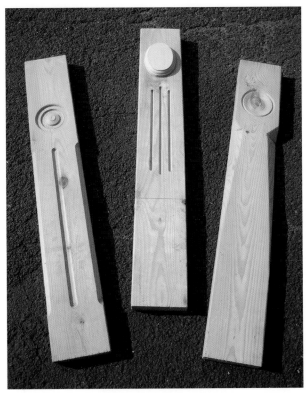

The chamfered edges, center veining, and inset rosettes on these post casings were decorated entirely using a router and router attachments.

Drill and Drill Press

A handheld **drill** is a must for a fence project. It is needed for drilling pilot holes for nails, bolts, and screws, and it is also useful for quickly driving those screws into your lumber. I always like to have two handheld drills with me on a project.

On top of its uses for fastening your fence components together, the handheld drill can also be a great decorating tool. Drilling small or shallow holes with a handheld drill is often easy and quick.

Most people don't think about the decorative aspects of a circle or a collection of overlapping circles, but a handheld drill can be a great decorating tool for making circles on your pickets.

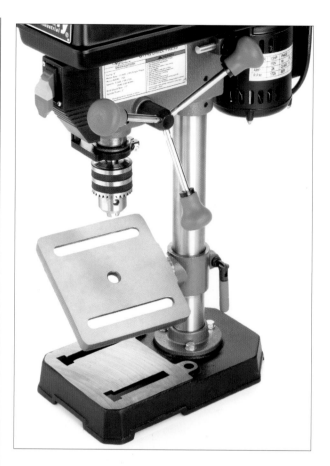

A **drill press** allows you to make holes with greater control and precision than you can make with a handheld drill. This can be important for larger, deeper holes that you might get noticeably crooked with a handheld drill.

Hand Tools

In addition to the power tools, there are numerous smaller hand tools that you are likely to use. There's a good chance that you own some or all of these tools.

- Chalk line—useful for marking long post runs and for making cut or attachment lines over several boards at once
- Clamps
- Clamshell hole digger—useful when holes are too deep for a spade shovel
- Combination, speed, or framing square
- Hammer
- Tape measures, rulers
- Metal auger bar—useful for breaking up compacted dirt and loosening rocks when digging holes
- Nail set—for sinking finishing nails
- Painting and finishing supplies—brushes, rollers, paint pads and other tools useful for painting
- Pencils and markers
- Plumb bob—for finding exact posthole locations
- Rope—to drape between two posts in order to find and mark a natural scallop
- Sandpaper
- Hand saws—useful for finishing blind/stop cuts with finer control than using a circular saw
- Spade shovel
- Spirit levels—used for keeping posts plumb during the setting process
- Spray paint or tent pegs—for marking exact post-hole locations
- Wrenches and ratchets

You can make holes at precise angles by adjusting the drill press table and clamping your lumber to the table. In addition to drilling holes, there are bits for drill presses that allow you to make decorative rosettes. These rosettes can adorn decorative fence posts or even individual pickets.

Choosing Materials

When choosing the types of lumber to construct your fence, give consideration to the style of your fence and what type of lumber will be the most attractive and economical to use in achieving it. If you want your fence to last a lifetime, the cheapest lumber may not be the most economical.

Lumber

Picket fences are often made from 1x or 1-inch stock. If the pickets will be relief sculptured, 2x material should be used. You can then cut relief work up to $1/2$ inch deep on one side, and the board will still maintain adequate strength to be a sturdy picket.

Lattice and plywood panels come in 4 x 8-foot sections. Pressure-treated lattice and exterior-grade plywood are available and should be used when constructing a fence. You can buy lattice slats or cut them from 2x material if you want to construct your own lattice with a different pattern.

Gridwork patterns are often constructed from 2x material. This material tends to give the fence strong ar-

chitectural characteristics—an attractive feature of the geometric grid-style fence.

In addition to lumber dimensions, consider the lumber treatments and species of wood that are available. Consider the types of synthetic lumber that you could use and determine if the initial cost would be worth the elimination of painting, staining, or sealing costs that you would accrue over the life of the fence.

While redwood and cedar have natural insect-repellant properties that make them popular choices for fence construction, they do not hold up well when in contact with the ground and moisture. For this reason, only fence rails and infill are typically made of these woods. For a durable post, it is necessary to use a lumber that will resist the attacks of fungus and insects.

An alternative is to use pressure-treated lumber, which is frequently made from widely available species of southern yellow pine on the East Coast and Douglas fir on the West Coast. This lumber is pressure cooked with chemicals to make it resistant to insects and decay. The wood is placed in a large container that is sealed and pressurized to force the chemical solution into the

Quality wooden fences look strong and appealing, even when they are weathered and worn after years of use. For your fence to look this good even when it is old, you need to start with good lumber.

wood fibers. The chemical solutions are designed to deter pests.

While pressure-treated lumber is decay-resistant for twenty or more years, it does have some drawbacks. Pressure-treated posts and boards that look fine in the lumberyard may become cracked and twisted after only six months to a year. Pressure-treated lumber is often shipped to building-supply stores and then purchased by the consumer while it is still wet. As the lumber dries it shrinks. If the outer portion of the lumber dries too quickly while the inner portion is plump and wet, the wood will crack. For this reason it is a good idea to apply a sealer that will inhibit the wood's ability to absorb and release moisture. The sealer will not prevent the release of moisture, but it will slow it down so the wood dries out more uniformly and cracking is reduced.

Pressure-treated lumber can be painted or stained, but you usually need to wait a period of time so that the water impregnated in the new wood has a chance to evaporate. If the wood is painted while there is still a good bit of moisture inside the lumber, the paint will fail as that moisture works its way out.

Posts of pressure-treated lumber are often cut from the center of the tree. This center-cut lumber is prone to splitting and twisting, even if it does dry out slowly. It can be very frustrating to go to a lumberyard and find nothing but center-cut posts that you know will crack and twist as they dry out.

Do not use inferior lumber that is full of cracks and defects. If it looks this bad before you buy it, imagine how it will look as it ages.

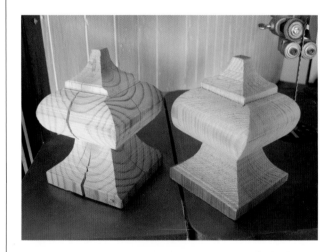

The finial on the left was made from wet, center-cut 4 x 4 lumber. As the lumber dried, the finial cracked and split. For the finial on the right, a higher-quality lumber was used, yielding much better results.

If you have the luxury of enough time and space, buy your pressure-treated lumber well before you begin your project to give it time to partially dry before you use it. That will allow you to discard posts that bend and split too severely before you secure them in the ground. By doing this, you can see which posts and what parts of them twisted. Keep your straightest posts for gates and other high-profile spots. For some of the posts, you can stick the twisted or warped end underground and leave the relatively straight end above.

You will want to make sure your pickets are not cut too thin; they need to have the strength to hold up to the bumps and knocks that a fence must be able to withstand. You do not want boards that are warped and cracked before you put them up. If you don't start with attractive materials, there is no way you will end up with an attractive fence.

Most lumberyards stock a higher-quality decking lumber, which is ¼ inch thicker than fence boards with only a slightly higher price. I strongly suggest spending the small bit of extra cash to make your pickets from quality decking lumber. They will look better, last longer, and give you fewer headaches than lower-quality lumber. The rounded edge on decking lumber will be an attractive feature of the uncut portions of your picket.

Another option is to buy untreated lumber direct from a mill and treat the lumber yourself. At a mill, you can typically get posts cut from other parts of the tree other than the center, and because they are not pressure treated, they are not saturated with water. Home-improvement stores carry wood-treating solutions that can be used on the entire post or just the portion that will go into the ground. Treating the wood yourself will yield straight, smooth posts with a longer lifespan.

This fence was made using decking lumber for the pickets. Full-sized patterns for the picket and gate scroll are included in the Patterns chapter.

Hardwoods such as black locust, white oak, and Osage orange are often available locally at a reasonable rate and provide adequate resistance to pests and fungi. Finding what woods are available and work well with ground contact in your area may not be easy for everyone, but for some people it can yield higher-quality posts at a lower cost.

Some imported woods, especially types from South America, are known for their ability to endure the harsh conditions of ground contact and exposure to the elements. Ipe, often called ironwood, is one family of trees that has increased in use as lumber in the twenty-first century, frequently in decking and fencing because of its ability to resist decay and insects. Many species of ipe are excellent choices for outdoor applications.

But, as the term ironwood implies, ipe is very hard, making it tougher on the blades and bits that are used to cut into it. Still, that toughness makes it the last choice of wood-boring insects.

Many of these South American hardwoods, which years ago were taken from the wild, are now cultivated to prevent forest depletion. You can check with your local supplier to confirm that their lumber comes from a managed, sustainable growth source.

Synthetic Materials

Not all synthetic lumber is made of the same type of plastic resin material. While all plastics are derived from fossil fuels, each type has distinct properties from being made through different procedures and having different additives strengthening and stabilizing them.

The most environmentally friendly form of plastic lumber is made of high-density polyethylene, often known by its initials HDPE. HDPE is a recyclable plastic used for milk jugs, shampoo bottles, and various other household containers. HDPE containers are stamped with a #2 recyclable symbol.

HDPE lumber scraps themselves are recyclable and can be melted down and used again to make more HDPE lumber. HDPE lumber is viewed as more environmentally friendly than other forms of synthetic lumber, which usually are more difficult to make from recycled materials and are more difficult to recycle themselves. Polystyrene and polypropylene are other forms of plastic that can be used to make lumber. There are very few manufacturers, however, using these resins to make lumber, so their availability is limited.

Cellular polyvinyl chloride, or cellular PVC, is another type of plastic used to make lumber. Not all PVC used in the building trade is classified as lumber. There are many building products in use that are made with PVC. Railing and fencing systems made from hollow regular PVC are common. These PVC systems and their components are not lumber. They cannot be sawn or molded and would be ruined if you tried to mold a decorative edge on them using your router.

Cellular PVC is different. It is extruded into many standard lumber sizes and molding profiles. It cuts similar to wood, and you can use your band saw and router on it and get good results without shattering the board. The process to make cellular PVC puts tiny air bubbles in the foam extrusion mix, making it less than half the weight and density of regular PVC. Cellular PVC tends to be among the most expensive forms of synthetic lumber; however, because of its ability to be molded into profiles, it is often practical to use for trim and detail work for fences.

Finally, not all synthetic lumber is 100 percent plastic resin. Plastic lumber tends to be more flexible than wood. This can make it difficult to use structurally. To make the lumber stiffer, manufacturers add fibers from wood, fiberglass, or other materials; these mixtures give the lumber more rigidity.

But let's face it: If something looks cheap, inferior, or fake, we say it looks plastic. Most of us don't have a problem with plastic lumber as long as it doesn't look anything like plastic. We want plastic to mimic a more desirable material. Sometimes plastic falls short of imitating wood. I grade plastic lumber appearance by the 100-10-1 rule. Some synthetic fences have a glossy balloon sheen that looks plastic from 100 feet away. Others are better, but at 10 feet away you can tell by the repeat of embossed patterns, seams, and joints that it's fake. The best ones look wooden even if you are less than an arm's length away.

Each manufacturer uses its own techniques and processes to create lumber products. Some produce very realistic lumber with the look of weathered stain, weathered paint, or fresh paint. Some are more believable as wood than others. It is a good idea to view samples of the lumber you intend to use for your project, so that you know if the appearance of the lumber is up to your standards.

Make sure all the plastic lumber you use has color running all the way through the material. That is helpful in two ways. First, it means you can cut and shape the lumber and it will have the same color as the uncut parts. Also, accidental gouges and scratches can be sanded down and made less noticeable.

Most manufacturers of synthetic lumber offer a variety of colors and some even offer custom colors. When you ask them if you can paint their product they usually ask you to consider buying the lumber in the color you want. That is good advice. If you really want to paint your lumber, find out what the manu-

The collar and necktie appliqués on this picket fence are made from cellular PVC that has been painted with house paint. Cellular PVC holds paint well with a bit of sanding to roughen the surface.

facturer suggests for paints that work on their products. HDPE lumber is noted for being difficult to paint. Conversely, I have had good results using primer and latex house paint on cellular PVC.

Most plastic lumber manufacturers state that their products cut and shape like real wood and that you can use woodworking tools on them in the same ways you use them for real wood. In my experience that is close to true.

When cutting plastic lumber with my table saw and circular saw, I saw no significant difference from wood. In fact, with the band saw I found that the plastics were actually easier to cut than real wood. Often when I am cutting a line almost parallel to the grain with a band saw, jigsaw, or scroll saw, the blade may want to follow the grain of the lumber and I will start to go off my cutting line and need to adjust. This is a problem that I never had in cutting any of the synthetics.

I found inconsistency with some of the thicker pieces of plastic lumber, which would sometimes have air bubbles near their centers. It did limit my ability to treat them like lumber. I could not cut and mold them like I could real wood.

Another minor drawback to plastic lumber is that the static cling of the plastic sawdust was stronger than the static cling of wood sawdust.

Plastic lumber does not have the rigidity of real wood. I found that using plastic lumber with fiberglass additives for the frame members did make a big difference. In cases where I used 100 percent plastic for the rails, I had to keep the fence sections shorter than 8 feet to avoid sagging. You can use this difference between plastic and wood lumber to your advantage. Some designs that feature curved lumber are actually easier to make with more flexible synthetic lumber than they are with real wood.

Gravel and Cement

For setting posts, you will frequently use both gravel and cement. If you are using plastic lumber you will not need gravel. One big advantage of using plastic over real wood is that the plastic will not rot. All that extra digging to lay down a layer of gravel for the drainage necessary to prevent rot is no longer a concern with plastic. Of course you will still use cement for firmly anchored posts, regardless of whether they are plastic or wooden.

Real Wood or Fake?

Many synthetics have come a long way in their ability to mimic wood. Only the gate at lower left is made of genuine wood.

Calculating Quantities

Just how many posts, rails, baseboards, pickets, post caps, post urns, nails, and bags of concrete will you need? Don't panic—we will handle each of these items one at a time. If you have a plan drawing of your fence, this task will be much easier.

Posts. Count the number of posts marked on your plan drawing. Determine the height above the ground and the depth below the ground you need the posts to be, and add these two figures together. This number is the length you need for each post.

Concrete. There are several options available. Although you can anchor your post in a cylinder of concrete to ground level, this is frequently an unnecessary burden. Much depends on what works for your geographic area, how deep you set your post, and whether or not the post is a gate post. I highly recommend at least some concrete for gate posts. Count the number of fence posts on the plan. Assume one bag of premix concrete for each posthole and two bags for each gate posthole. When using wood, use gravel with concrete. Put a layer of gravel on the bottom, followed by a layer made from one bag of premixed concrete around the post. After the concrete dries, fill the hole using the rocks and dirt you removed when digging the hole. For gate posts, use two bags of concrete and complete with dirt.

Stringers. Multiply the number of posts by the number of stringers you will have between two posts—probably two stringers. This gives you the total number of stringers you will need. Some of these stringers may be different lengths, and the distance between gate posts may be different than the distances between other posts. Group the sections by length and figure how many stringers you need for each.

Baseboards. Follow the same procedure used to calculate stringers. Multiply the number of posts by the number of baseboards you will have between two posts. If your posts are not evenly spaced, calculate the number of odd-size baseboards in each length group.

Infill. To calculate most infill, pickets, plain boards, lattice, and grid patterns, determine the amount of lumber necessary to complete one section, then multiply those lumber needs by the number of sections. Again, if you have several section lengths, you must perform this exercise for each group.

If you use additional moldings for posts or appliqués, you will need to estimate those lumber dimensions as well. Finally, allow for some spoilage, cutting errors, lumber defects, and last-minute changes that may require additional lumber. You may want to purchase 10 percent more lumber than you expect to use if picking up the extra lumber on an as-needed basis will be inconvenient.

Nails and Screws

Larger nails and screws provide more of a bite to hold your components together. Always go for the longest nails or screws that will not poke through the other side of your lumber. I strongly recommend using screws, so that repositioning and later repairs, replacements, and general maintenance are easier.

If you are making your fence from high-quality synthetic lumber or a highly decay-resistant wood species, it is reasonable to presume that your fence could last your lifetime. For your fence to last a long time, you need to choose nails that will resist rust or not rust at all. Galvanized nails are covered with a thin, electroplated layer of rust-resistant material. The layer is so thin that it is easily damaged during installation, and the nails begin to rust almost immediately. For that reason, I suggest spending a bit more money on better fasteners with greater rust resistance.

Nails and screws that are dipped in a rust-resistant metal have a thicker coating than galvanized nails. They are less likely to flake or chip during installation and will last for many years. The cost of these nails and screws is somewhat higher than that of galvanized

This fence is simple but attractive. Most of the pickets on this fence are still in shape. Screws would have made it easy to replace the two that are damaged. Unfortunately the rusty nails on this fence will probably give out before the lumber does.

A handle makes it easy to pull a gate open or closed.

nails, but their performance is well worth the price. Frequently they will last a decade or longer, but eventually they will start to rust.

Still better than galvanized or coated nails and screws are those made of stainless steel or aluminum. Damage caused to these nails during installation or by many years of use will not affect their rust resistance. These nails and screws cost far more than the coated, however, so people tend to avoid them when making large projects.

The fasteners you choose will need to last the lifetime of your fence lumber. Determine how long you want your fence to last and choose your fasteners accordingly.

Latches and Hinges

There are a number of latches and locks available for keeping gates secured in the open or closed position. Choose those with the ability to stand up to the use and abuse they will receive. If you do not need your gate to latch closed, you may still want to add a simple handle you can use to pull the gate open.

When choosing hinges, keep in mind that the most important factor is their ability to firmly attach to both your gate and the post. Purchase large heavy-duty hinges and extra-long bolts to make a strong, long-lasting gate. Do not be afraid to use a hefty set of hinges. Dainty is not "in" when it comes to gate hinges. A gate that sags on bent hinges will be a constant irritant each time it is opened.

Many hinges are available with a spring mechanism that allows the gate to be self-closing. Use them where appropriate. This feature is very handy for gates that are opened frequently.

Choose appropriate bolts or screws to use with your hinges. Small bolts or screws can be pulled out of the post or gate after only a modest amount of activity. Use hinges secured with very large bolts or several moderately large bolts. Long, thick bolts will grasp the post and gate firmly, ensuring a lengthy service life for your gate.

Choosing Hinges

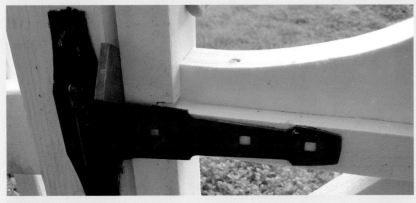

T-hinge

Strap hinge

Strap hinge

Above: heavy-duty straps; right: automatic-closing hinge

T-hinges extend the point of contact up and down the post, helping to support the gate. T-hinges can be purchased with hidden spring closures that automatically close the gate.

Strap hinges are another popular choice. It is often a good idea to buy long lag bolts to use on the post to give your strap hinge a better hold.

This strap hinge is attached with a thick heavy-duty screw that goes deep into the post. The end of the screw contains a peg for the barrel of the strap hinge to slip over.

Heavy-duty straps on these hinges extend far across the rails of the fence. Coupled with a sturdy frame, extra-strong hinges help this gate stay square without diagonal bracing.

This **automatic-closing hinge** forces the gate to rise up as it is opened; gravity then pulls the gate back down to close it when it is released.

Posts, Foundations, and Framing

In order for your fence to remain stable and erect year after year, you need to start with strong posts and a good foundation.

Strength and Longevity Considerations

Drainage, wind, and use will impact the longevity and serviceability of your fence's posts. Posts are the hardest part of the fence to replace so of course you want them to last.

Drainage

Keeping fence posts dry at all times is not practical, but keeping them as dry as possible and allowing them to shed, resist, and drain off excess water will greatly increase their longevity. Fungus, termites, and other insects will reduce the lifespan of wooden posts. Providing excellent drainage for your posts will make it harder for living organisms to feed on them.

The end grain at the top of your post is the most susceptible to absorbing moisture. For that reason it is a good idea to cut your post tops with angles that direct rainwater to run off. After you cut your post tops, you should apply a paint, stain, or clear sealant over the top to help further protect it from moisture. An even better option is to apply a post cap to the top of each post. A simple block cap will protect your post and is easy to replace if it is damaged.

The underground portions of posts will rot if they are constantly in water-saturated earth. To allow post bottoms to dry quickly after each rain, set them in holes filled with crushed and compacted gravel. The gravel allows for drainage and does not trap moisture as earth and concrete do. Another advantage to posts set in gravel is that they can be dug out more easily than posts set with concrete if they need to be replaced.

Although setting posts in gravel usually provides satisfactory support for line posts, gate posts should be set using concrete. Gate posts need to endure the tugging, twisting torque from the weight and swing of the gate. If the gate post starts to shift from these forces, the gate will not open and close properly.

Posts, however, should not be set completely encased in concrete. The lower six inches of the post should be nestled in twelve inches of gravel to allow for drainage.

Wind

Wind, or wind combined with rain, can also cause a fence footing to fail. Wind is not usually an issue for the typical garden or front yard fence. However, tall privacy fences will need to stand up to substantial wind

Post Anchoring Systems

The most backbreaking, painful part of creating a fence is setting the posts. And the most painful part of maintaining a fence is replacing a broken off or rotten post. A failed post that was set using a good bit of concrete can be quite a chore to remove from the ground. That is why some companies have developed anchoring systems that allow for easier replacement of damaged posts. Most of these systems involve either a socket or a pin that connects the post to the anchoring system.

In the socket method, the post is usually the full length it would be if set in a traditional method. The post is set in some kind of concrete or metal anchor in the ground, with a means to release the post from the anchoring system should the post fail.

In the pin method, a concrete footing has an iron rebar pin (or set of pins) that extends above ground. A hole is drilled into the base from the bottom of the post to allow the post to be slipped over the rebar pin.

Setting metal posts in concrete foundation walls is one way to avoid replacing wood posts, but because the posts do not match the infill, the posts can be placed behind the infill and with the post tops lower than the infill to minimize their visibility.

Although gravel is preferred for line posts, gate posts should be set mostly in concrete, to allow for adequate drainage and withstand the force of frequent opening and closing. Gate posts should still have a base of gravel for proper drainage.

force. Greater post depth and increased use of concrete will reduce the chances of fence failure. Placing one-third of the post length in the ground is a good rule to follow to prevent this type of failure.

Use and Abuse

Fences frequently receive a good deal of use and abuse. They may have heavy objects leaned against them, they are used as bench seats, and even walked upon in some cases.

But gates have it worse. Gates are used several times a day. All that opening, closing, slamming, and pulling exerts force on the supporting posts and the gate itself. Because of the heavy use, gate posts must be set deeply and anchored with concrete.

Setting the Posts

To make a perfectly straight line of posts, use string to mark the outline of the fence on the property. To sup-

port the string use either stakes or batter boards. Batter boards are constructed of two vertical stakes with one horizontal board attached between the two stakes. Batter boards will be more work to construct, but you will be able to move the string along the top rail. With stakes you will need to reposition them until you get it right.

Start by placing a batter board or a stake *past* the location for each corner post. Stretch a line between them, making the line taut. If the distance is too great to keep the line taut, place an intermediate batter board or stake between the corner ones and use it to help stretch the line.

Next, measure along the line and plant a stake or paint an X for each intermediate posthole. Then dig holes with at least a 12-inch diameter at each location.

Depth

Ideally, you want your post bottoms placed below the frost line. Freezing ground will attempt to expand, putting pressure on your posts in all directions. If the ground freezes below your post, it can push your post upward as it expands. Placing your post below the lowest point of ground freeze for your area will mean only the sides of your posts are pressed by the freezing ground, but the bottom will not be pushed up. The upward pressure of frost heaves typically does damage to fences by lifting posts, pulling apart the framing as it lifts. Contact your municipal building inspection department to find the local code or recommendations for your area.

A good rule is to set your post at least 30 inches deep for regular posts and 36 inches deep for gate and corner posts. Another guideline is that one-third of the total post length should be underground, so if your fence will have 7-foot-high posts, then 2 feet, 4 inches should be below ground.

The rule for minimum post depth is at least one-fourth of the post's total length or 2 feet deep, whichever is greater. This means a 6-foot-high fence would use, at the very shortest, 8-foot posts sunk 2 feet. But even a 4-foot-high fence should still use posts that are sunk at least 2 feet.

I do not recommend using the minimum. Sometimes a large rock or other encumbrance will limit your ability to dig a given hole to the full depth. In those cases you might be forced to go with this less desirable alternative. The truth is there are no guarantees that going to a given depth or using a given amount of concrete will always work. On rare occasions, areas of poor drainage, unexpected hard winters, and other special conditions will prevail over even the best practices.

So, if your posts are longer than you need them to be (they often are if you buy 4 x 4 x 8 posts), sink some of that extra length under the ground. The added depth will help make the posts more secure.

Foundations

Posts can be set in an earth and rocks foundation, an earth and gravel foundation, a solid concrete and gravel foundation, or a foundation that uses layers of these elements. Generally speaking, the more concrete used, the sturdier the post foundation. Set gate posts and corner posts with at least some concrete, since

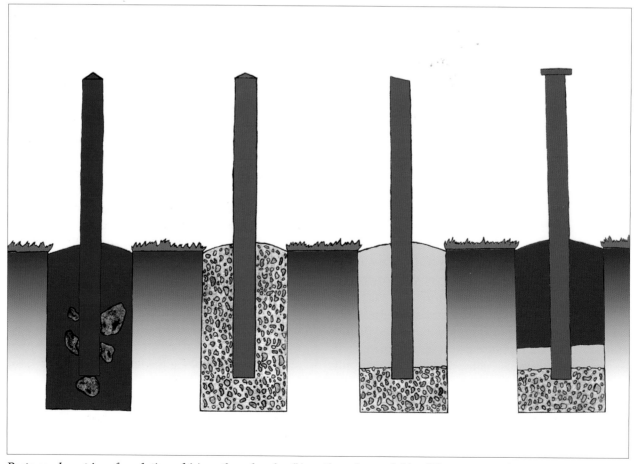

Posts can be set in a foundation of (a) earth and rocks, (b) earth and gravel, (c) solid concrete and gravel, or (d) layers of all these elements.

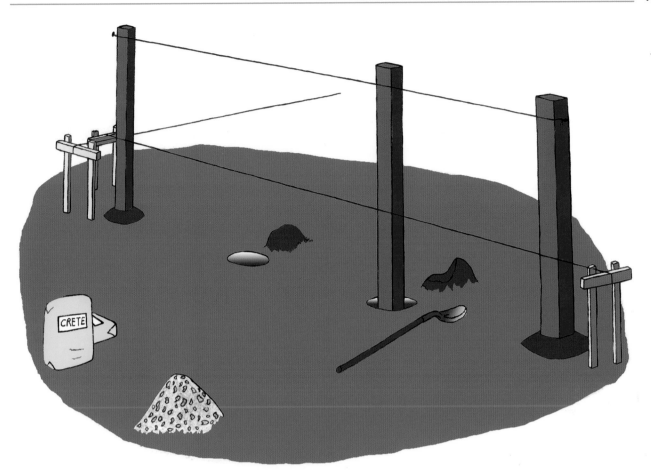

To perfectly align a row of posts, set the corner post first. Then string a line around the top and bottom of the corner posts. Then begin setting intermediate posts. Position and set the posts so they are just flush with, but not pressing, the lines.

these posts receive extra stress and heavy use. All wooden posts should be set with the bottom 6 inches of the post nestled in 1 foot of gravel.

The gravel is used to ensure drainage away from the bottom of the post, thus inhibiting decay. Gravel and earth should be added slowly and then tamped thoroughly to remove any air pockets. If rubble is used to extend concrete, the concrete-rubble mixture also should be tamped to remove air pockets.

Alignment

Often you will have a long, straight stretch that you would like to keep perfectly aligned. While some can do this by eye, others like to have a method that will ensure a straight line of posts in a run. The following method works well for achieving near-perfect alignment.

Set corner posts first. Use two spirit levels placed on adjacent sides of the post. One person should hold the post level while the other adds and tamps the gravel and earth and then pours the concrete. Bracing the posts with pieces of 2 x 4 may be necessary to keep the posts level while the concrete is setting. Use two spirit levels placed on adjacent sides of the post to help keep posts in plumb while setting. Position the post flush

with, but not pressing against, the lines between the two corner posts.

Once corner posts are securely set, hammer two nails about 1 inch deep into the outer sides of each post, one near the top of the post, the other more toward the bottom. Tie a line to the top nail. Pull the line around the side of the post; attach the line to the top nail on the far side of the second corner post. Make certain the line is tight. Do the same for the lower nails.

You could also continue to use your batter boards or stakes for the lower lines. The benefit to using your batter boards is that you would not need to deface the lower portion of your post with an unnecessary hole, a hole that you cannot cut off when you trim the post to its final height.

Begin setting intermediate posts. Position the posts so that they are just flush with, but not pressing, the lines between the two corner posts. Use two spirit levels to help you adjust the posts to plumb. Add footing matter and tamp thoroughly. Stake the posts to keep them plumb, with supports if necessary, as the concrete sets. Often when setting posts with concrete and earth, the earth will hold the posts in place until the concrete sets.

Frame-to-Post Attachment

There are a number of ways that you can attach frame members to the post. For some designs, the top rail runs over the post top, providing a large area to make the attachment with screws or nails. Other designs will have the rails in front of the post, again giving a large surface area to screw the rail to the post. If the post is dado cut to receive the rail, the attachment will be even more secure.

Top right: The easiest way to attach the frame between the posts is to toe nail or toe screw the rails to the post. This provides a weak connection that is prone to separation, as seen here. Right: When the post is dado cut to receive the nail, the attachment is more secure.

Posts and Frames Checklist

■ Contact local building department. Here you'll find information you need for permission to build your fence. They will inform you of structural and appearance guidelines. It's best to know your local requirements before you begin construction.

■ Contact utilities. Know where buried lines are before you begin to dig. Utility companies will come to your house and mark underground lines and pipes so you can build safely.

■ Put post bottoms below the frost line. Frost heave can lift posts out of the ground, tearing apart your fence, so learn how far down the frost line is and make sure the post bottoms are below it.

■ Put post bottoms as deep as possible. Even if frost heave is not an issue, deeper is still better. The deeper your post is in the ground, the more secure it will be. Place your posts as deep as you reasonably can.

■ Set posts in gravel. Water is the enemy of wood posts and causes decay. Posts set in a base of gravel will survive longer, because the water will drain better.

■ Use concrete for gate posts. Because gates are frequently used, they need more support. Soil conditions and post depth will also dictate if concrete should be used for all posts.

■ Secure the post-to-rail connection. Toeing with either screws or nails is the least secure method of attaching rails to posts. Consider using one of the many other methods for making secure frame attachments.

■ Use screws. Long screws will have a better bite on the lumber than short nails. Use the longest screws you can that will not poke through the back of your lumber. Choose rust-resistant screws that will last for the life of your lumber.

Toeing

The most common and attractive way to place the frame members is between the posts. This presents a bit of a problem. The easiest way to attach the frame between posts is often to toe nail or screw the rails to the post. Even with long screws, this provides a weak connection. It is prone to problems and is high maintenance to keep attached. But fortunately there are alternatives to toeing.

Stringer Hangers

Specialized metal brackets called stringer hangers are made for placing rails between two uprights. These brackets do a pretty good job of holding the post and rails together. What is more, if a fence section is damaged and needs to be replaced, it is simple to unscrew a few lock-in screws from the holes on the side of the stringer hanger and lift the section out.

The downside to stringer hangers is that they are metal. If you are painting the fence a solid color, you can paint your stringer hangers the same color and they will be hard to notice. If you leave your fence natural or use a transparent stain on your wood, the stringer hangers would be more visible. They are usually small and not that noticeable even when left unpainted. But, if stringer hangers do not sound satisfactory to you, there are more options.

Cleats

Cleats are usually blocks placed below the rails to support the weight of the rails. The blocks are then securely attached to the post with screws. The rail is often toed to the post to hold it in place from lateral pressure, but the downward weight would be supported by the

Attachment with stringer hangers.

Above top: Cleats are used to support the weight of the rails.
Above bottom: Attachment with cleats.

cleat. Cleats are usually pretty strong and dependable ways to hold up the infill and they are easy to install. Sound perfect?

The downside of wood cleats is that they usually need to be big to keep from being split by the screws in them and the weight of the fence pressing down on them. This makes them bulky looking. This isn't that noticeable for the lower rail, but for upper rails it can detract from the overall appearance of the fence.

On the upside, synthetic materials allow you to make cleats that look smaller and more decorative. Small cleats made from synthetics will take screws and weight without splitting and breaking apart. But what if you are not making your fence from a synthetic lumber?

Stiles

Stiles are vertical boards attached to the post and used to support the rails and infill of the fence, making a sturdier attachment. Several screws or nails can be used to fasten the stile securely to the post. Often a picket from the infill can be used as a stile. A small block of lumber in the post can also make a discreet attachment for rails.

Above top: A block of lumber on the post serves as a stile in this fence. Above bottom: Here a picket attached to the post functions as a stile.

Pointed and Beveled Post Tops

Tool required: Table saw

The table saw is a great tool for cutting beveled tops. Bevels can be cut to overlap each other at a central point to form a pyramid, or you can cut four slanted sides with a flat top.

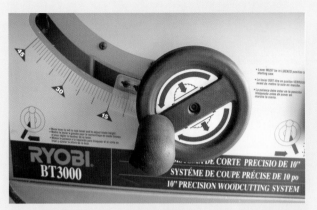

Adjust the blade to the desired angle.

Check the height of the blade perpendicular to the table. It must be at least half the width of the post.

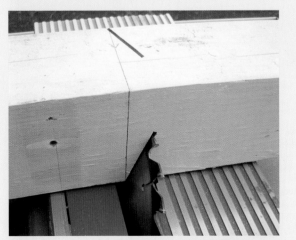

Draw a line all around the wood to mark the base of the pyramid you will cut. Use your crosscut sled or sliding miter guide to cut the post. The bottom of the blade should be aligned with the pencil line. After the first pass, turn the post to cut the next side.

After the third cut, the excess lumber on top will separate from the post.

Turn the post to cut the fourth side.

Here is the finished post.

Raised-Panel Post Cap

Tool required: Table saw with tenoning jig

It would be dangerous to try to use your rip fence to cut bevels on the top of a post cap. The tenoning jig slides parallel to the blade, like the crosscut sled or miter guide, while its clamp holds the lumber tight near the blade instead of your fingers.

Adjust your table saw blade to the desired angle.

Secure the square post cap in the clamp of the tenoning jig.

Check the height of the blade perpendicular to the table for the width of the post cap you plan to remove. If you remove 2 inches from all four sides of a 7$\frac{1}{2}$-inch post cap, you will be left with a 3$\frac{1}{2}$-inch platform at the top of the post cap.

Using the tenoning jig, pass the post cap through the blade four times, turning it to the next face after each pass.

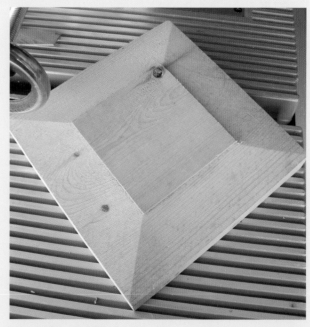

Here is the completed post cap.

Above: A stile to support the infill is fastened to the post with nails.

Post Belts and Encased Post

A post belt is basically a decorative cleat that wraps all the way around the outside of your post. It can be made of boards or moldings. The rails then rest on top of the belts. The belt works like a cleat on the sides of the post and like a decoration on the front of the post. Posts can also be encased in lumber. Openings in that encasement can be used to receive rails or rails and stiles. The lower part of the encasement below the rail acts as a cleat.

Above: Post belts support the rail and are also decorative. Right: This stringer has had a rabbet joint cut on the end so that it securely fastens to the post corner stile and rests on the post's panel rail.

Dado Joints

If you want simple posts, unbelted and not encased, it is also possible to use dado joints between posts; however, this would be taking away wood on two sides of the posts to make the dados, and 4 x 4 posts do not have a great deal of wood to spare. So it does weaken the post and it is bit of work.

Mortise and Tenon Joints

Mortise and tenon joints are common in informal split rail fencing. Mortise holes are placed through the post, and rail ends act as the tenon inserted in the mortised hole. Mortise and tenon joints work well for this fencing because the mortise holes can be cut oversized and loose, allowing for easy assembly with tapered end rails.

For more formal fence styles, a more precise mortise hole should be cut. Mortises for picket fences should

Left: Rounded mortise holes in posts are common for rustic post and rail fences. Below left and right: Mortises, rectangular holes cut into posts, can be used to securely hold rails.

have rectangular openings to receive rectangular rail ends. You can only drill a circle; you cannot drill a rectangular shape into the side of a post. Some people are willing to drill a series of smaller holes in the general shape of a rectangle and use a chisel to chip out the remaining wood. This level of work often precludes the mortise and tenon from being used in more formal fencing.

Special Cases

Most of us do not have perfectly flat yards on barren square lots. Many yards have trees, boulders, slopes, curves, dips, and mounds—all obstacles that the fence builder must overcome.

Trees

Trees in the fence line must be handled carefully. Attaching your fence to a tree can make it susceptible to disease. If the tree does not become diseased and die, it will continue to grow and expand, and as it does, it will distort and pull at your fence. Your fence should stop short of the tree to allow the tree to live and grow. It is best to remove obstacles when possible.

Above: Allowing ample space between your fence and a tree will allow the tree to move and grow without damaging your fence.

Left: Trees keep moving and growing throughout their lives. Cutouts that are just large enough for the tree today will be too small tomorrow. The tree will push and pull at the fence and you will need to do frequent maintenance. These cutouts became inadequate and the trees have already begun their damage.

Slopes

Fencing a slope is probably the most common obstacle fence builders need to hurdle. If the terrain is particularly uneven, the sharp horizontal lines of a baseboard will draw attention to the unevenness of the land. There are several approaches to fencing a slope, each with advantages and drawbacks.

Stepped Infill and Frame

Stepped-frame fences have stringers hung perpendicular to the posts. In that sense, the construction of this type of fence is the same as that of a basic fence. It differs, however, in that the ends of the stringers on the uphill side of the fence section are closer to the earth than the ends on the downhill side. This type of construction has the appearance of steps, thus the term stepped frame. Such fences look best and are most practical on gradual slopes.

Right: To fence a hillside, you can use a sloping frame with sloping infill, a stepped frame with stepped infill, or a stepped frame with sloping infill. Below: Stepped infill and frame fences look best and are most practical on gradual slopes.

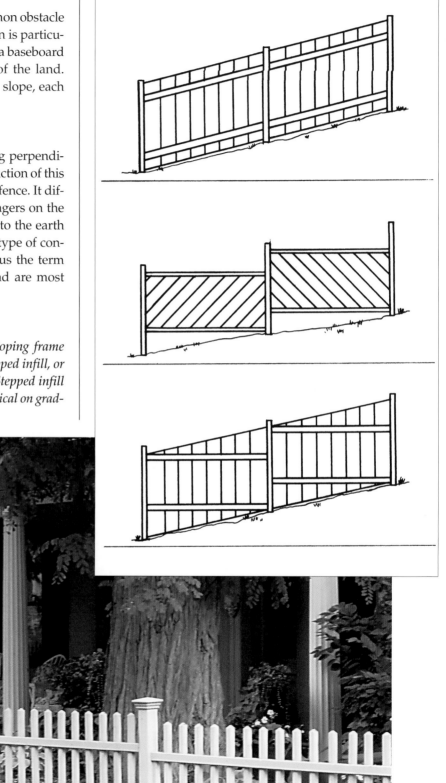

Sloped infill and frame fences are usually the best choice for steep slopes. They are easy to make with spaced pickets and leave no gaps at the base of the fence on the downhill side.

On steep slopes, there will be huge, triangular gaps between the fence bottom and the ground. Such gaps can appear unsightly and reduce the fence's ability to provide privacy and security. Sometimes using a kickboard cut to match the slope can be a good method of closing that gap.

Stepped frames are usually the best choice for geometric grid, panel, and lattice fences. They also work for picket, stockade, and baluster fences.

Sloping Frameworks

Sloping framework fences have stringers hung parallel to the earth. This type of fence is well suited to traverse either gradual or steep slopes. The end of each stringer must be cut at an angle so that it fits the post snugly.

Attach-on infill, such as a picket, is easily applied to the sloped frame, but infill that is inserted in the frame is not as easily used, especially if the grade is steep.

Conventional-sized lattice and panels may not be available to fit using only one piece between each section. Geometric grid patterns will need some alterations on the slope, but if well designed, such alterations will greatly increase the beauty of the fence and display the designer's creativity and adaptability.

Stepped Frame with Sloping Infill

The stepped frame, in which stringers are placed perpendicular to the posts, is easier to construct than the sloping frame, because stringers do not need to be miter-cut to fit each section. It is also stronger, because the length of the perpendicular stringers is shorter than that of a stringer placed parallel to the earth. As mentioned before, stepped frames leave large triangular voids along the bottom of the fence. To cover these voids, the infill is extended below the stringers on the bottom side of the slope and above the stringers on the top side.

Infill

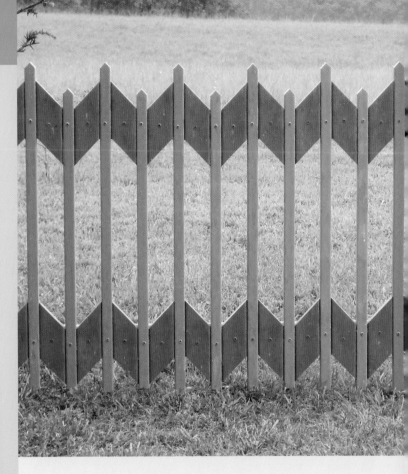

Infill is the material used to "fill in" the fence between the posts. In a picket fence, the pickets themselves are the infill. This chapter gives you an overview of the steps necessary to make your own spectacular infill. Reviewing the steps will help you put these tasks into perspective. You will find this useful as you design, assemble, and erect the pieces of your fence.

There are two basic types of infill: *mounted*, or attached on the rails; and *inset*, between a frame of rails and stiles. Mounted infill is easier, not requiring precision-cut lumber that fits perfectly inside a frame.

With mounted infill, if one picket is cut ½ inch longer than the others, it would not affect the integrity of the frame. You might notice one picket looks a bit higher than the rest. But with inset infill, if one baluster is too long, it will cause a rail or stile to bulge, if you are even able to get the baluster in the frame.

Mounted Infill

You can assemble mounted infill in creative ways.

Spaced Pickets

This is the easiest fence to assemble. It doesn't matter whether the pickets have just simple points or decoratively cut tops and bodies, the method of attachment is the same. Different picket patterns may take differing amounts of time to cut out, but they are all just as easy to hang as a basic stockade picket.

Pre-measure and mark the rails for picket placement. You may also want to make a *spacer*, a board to place between the pickets as you attach them so that you can space them apart evenly. To make a spacer, simply cut a board to the desired width.

If you find your fence posts are not quite evenly spaced, you can make up for it by altering the spacing of the last few pickets on the ends of the rows, adding or subtracting a quarter inch between the pickets to hide the distance.

Explore the vast array of picket patterns that are available for spaced picket fences. There are so many beautiful and varied styles to choose from, and you can make a breathtaking fence that will be simple to put together.

Alternating Pickets

Another option for adding visual interest is to alternate between two or three pickets with different widths, heights, or designs. Using more than one type of picket, however, adds a level of complexity to the work of laying out your pattern on the rails.

Closed Pickets

Closed-space pickets are pickets that abut on the rails with only a slight space between them for lumber expansion due to temperature and humidity changes. These fences take a bit more work to assemble effectively compared to spaced pickets. They require more pickets to fill a section of fence than the same-sized spaced pickets, and they require greater forethought to fit the pickets neatly between the posts. Closed pickets come in three varieties: symmetrical, mirrored, and picket and separator.

Which fence was easier to assemble? The answer may surprise you. The natural-finish fence was easier to assemble than the white one. The white fence was assembled with three different length pickets and this required some calculation. Each fence section had to begin and end with two long pickets next to the post. Although the natural-finish fence has more detailed pickets, it was easier to install since there is only one kind.

Above: Very simple picket designs can be made more visually appealing by alternating between one broad, pointed picket and two narrow, flat-topped pickets. Right: The pickets on this fence are all the same. The mirrored design effect is achieved by flipping every other picket to the opposite side.

Symmetrical closed-space pickets have, as the name implies, symmetrical sides. If you took the picket's paper pattern and folded it in half, both sides would be the same. Symmetrical closed-space pickets are frequently used to make privacy fences. They provide a good bit of visual blockage if the picket bodies have no, or only small, cutouts.

Mirrored Pickets

With this design, each opposing picket includes a cutout design that mirrors itself. In other words, the cutout design abuts its identical half in reverse and together they form a larger design. Each picket in the fence is the same, but when you assemble them on the rails you will flip every other picket as you go to accomplish the design.

In the pickets and separators approach, decorative separators are attached to the top and bottom rails.

Pickets and Separators

In this style, the pickets are applied in a way similar to a spaced picket fence. To make the fence more visually appealing, decorative short pickets, or *separators*, are attached between each picket, one to the top rail and the other to the bottom rail. Color can be used effectively with this style. You can paint the separators in a different color from the pickets to give the separators more accent. If you paint the pickets and separators the same color, you will create the illusion of a solid panel with cutouts.

Inset Infill

Another alternative, although more complicated, is to create a frame to inset the infill. Here are some options.

It can be difficult to classify a fence. With its long top rail and oversized baseboard, the fence at right looks like a balustrade fence. But taking a closer look you can see there are three types of pickets used: one style for the long picket that attaches to both the top and bottom rail, another rounded style for the separator that attaches to the top rail, and a third pointed style for the separator that attaches to the lower rail.

Baluster

A *baluster* is an ornamental upright post that gives support to a rail. A series of these posts forms a *balustrade*. This infill is among the most formal of all fence styles. Spaced balusters can feature either turned, flat-sawn, or square balusters. Closed baluster fences, with no spacing between balusters, are almost always made from flat-sawn pickets.

Baluster fences are usually accented by decoratively molded top and bottom rails and ornate baseboards. Balusters with round ends can be inserted in holes that are drilled into the stringers. Square-topped balusters and sawn balusters are often inserted into channels to hold them in place on the top stringer. Sometimes the bottom stringer is sloped to one side or beveled on two sides, like a gabled roof, to encourage water drainage. The baluster bottoms are then angled or notched to fit the bottom stringer.

This fence plate from a mid-nineteenth-century architectural details pattern book displays a selection of ornamental fence styles. Figures 1, 2, and 3 are sawn picket fences. Figures 4 and 7 feature two ornamental sawn baluster fences; Figure 7 also displays an ornamental sawn running trim across its top rail. Figure 5 features a grid-style fence with oversized post and ball. Figure 6, the most lavish and costly, is highlighted by six-inch round balusters that are both turned and carved.

An upper row of spaced square balusters in this fence tops a second row of unspaced sawn balusters.

Gradually Deepening Chamfer

Tools required: Circular saw and hand saw

A chamfer is a furrow you can make for decorating posts and post casings.

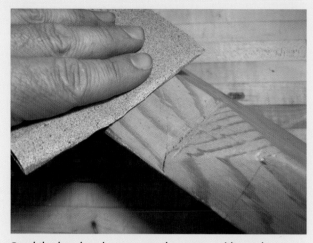

Sand the handmade cuts near the corner with a palm sander and then finish the corner itself by hand.

Draw the outline of the chamfer on the post. Adjust the circular saw to a 45-degree angle. Secure the board in a vise and cut one angle of the chamfer. Flip the board a quarter turn and cut the other angle of the chamfer.

Since the circular saw blade cuts in an arc, it will not completely cut the chamfer. Use a handsaw to finish the cut.

Here is the finished gradually deepening chamfer.

Grid and Panel

The beauty of a grid-and-panel fence is determined not by how ornate its pattern is, but rather by how well its pattern is planned. The pattern should fit neatly between the posts of the fence. Each section between posts should be symmetrically balanced.

Unlike most picket fences, grid-and-panel fences are very sensitive to changes in height and width. For this reason, it is important for you to make a scale drawing of a section of fence. You will use this drawing to determine the exact post spacing necessary to achieve a fence that is balanced in appearance.

Frequently with grid and panel style fences, the infill is constructed on a flat surface, like a driveway, in advance. This means that when the frame is applied to the fence, the infill as already attached to it. However, these fences are more difficult to customize to special circumstances like slopes and uneven terrain, so they are less frequently created by the do-it-yourselfer.

The strong geometric shapes of this Chippendale grid fence are striking. These grids are among the most tedious to construct, and thus they are rare to find.

It can be difficult to modify a grid design for varying height needs and slopes, but the designer of this fence was able to meet both challenges admirably.

Rosette Inlays

Rosettes can be made with routers or drill presses using special attachments.

Using a Router with a Trammel Guide Attachment

To make the rosette, mark the center on the post and drill a pilot hole, which will receive the trammel pin.

The trammel pin allows you to spin the router in a perfect circle. Insert the pin in the pilot hole and pivot the router around the pin. By adjusting the length of the trammel pin arm you can increase and decrease the radius of the circles you make.

By adjusting the depth setting on your router you make some surfaces of the rosette deeper than others. This classic bit was used on a deep setting to form the deepest circle of the rosette.

When your rosette is completed, you will need to use wood filler on the pilot hole you created to accommodate the trammel pin.

Using a Drill Press with a Rosette Cutter

Most drill presses permit you to vary the speed of the machine by allowing you to select from multiple pulley sizes. Use the slowest setting when making decorative rosettes with a rosette cutter.

Rosette cutters have the entire profile of the rosette in the blade of the cutting head. You slowly depress the cutting head into the lumber, and when you lift, the rosette is complete.

This rosette is perfectly inset to its post casing.

Combination

Combination fences use two or more styles of infill to form the fence design. These fences are usually more decorative and their construction is more complex. Generally, a fence can combine pales, pickets, and broad boards without significantly increasing the construction complexity. The assembly of these three types of infill is basically the same, because all three are typically nailed onto the stringers.

The infill of grid-and-panel and baluster fences, on the other hand, is often inset in the frame. Fences that combine a baluster or grid and panel design with pales, pickets, or boards are usually the most time-consuming, because they require the assembly of two or more types of infill.

Infill-to-Frame Attachment

Infill is predominantly either nailed or screwed to the frame. In some instances with panels of lattice, it may be set in channels. Using nails is often touted as the fastest way to attach infill. That may be true, but if a picket is damaged and needs to be replaced, it is much easier to remove without hurting the rest of the fence if it was attached with screws.

Infill that is attached to the side of rails is the most common type of infill for the do-it-yourselfer. This can be done on a flat surface before the rails are attached to the posts, but often this is done when the rails are up on the posts.

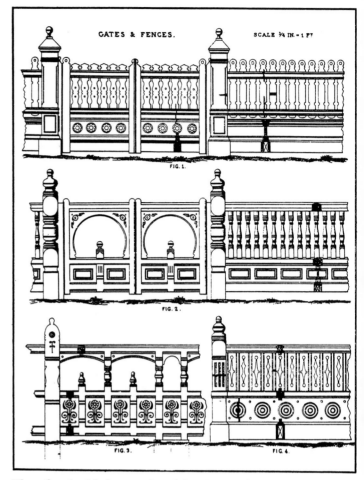

These four lavish fence styles of the nineteenth century illustrate a variety of designs achieved through the use of different combinations of gate, fence, and ornament detail. Figure 1 is a sawn picket fence with a double-door gate and high molded baseboard. Figure 2 is a combination fence with decoratively sawn balusters resting over a raised panel baseboard. Figure 3 is a grid-and-panel style fence with ornately carved and stenciled panel inserts. Figure 4 is a sawn baluster fence with a rosette-clad baseboard.

Gates

They open, they close. This is the primary function of gates, what all homeowners want their gates to do. They sag, they stick. No one wants this to happen to their gates, yet it often does. Before we examine how to construct a gate, we will examine why gates fail. This will help you understand why certain gate elements perform well and why certain gates last long.

Gates, especially large and heavy ones, can cause the holding post to start leaning. Bracing the post at the top prevents this. Braces can be utilitarian bars or decorative arches.

Gates are just fence sections, usually shorter than regular fence sections, so they should be lighter and less stressful to posts than a full fence section, right? Wrong.

Fence sections are nailed, screwed, or fixed to a post in some way to make an immovable bond. You cannot do that with a gate. Gates need to open and close freely on their hinges. Hinges are a frequent point of gate failure. Small hinges will often stress and break after only a short period of service. Another drawback to small hinges is that they usually use small screws.

This poses a problem for gates, because gates are opened and closed, and even slammed, repeatedly. All that jarring will cause tiny hinges to wear and screws to let loose their grip or sheer off completely.

But hinges are not the only source of gate failure. Gate frames themselves can become loose and shaky, sagging with age. Because gates are supported only on one side, the unsupported side will have a tendency to drop over time. This can be very frustrating to a homeowner that recently built a gate that hasn't been used long and hard, yet it has already begun dragging on the sidewalk or sticking against the post. Gate frames need to be extremely strong to prevent sagging.

Gates also frequently fail at the post. The post can twist and bend from the slamming and weight placed on it by the gate and the gate's movement. Your gate may begin to stick on the non-hinge side and you may think the gate itself is sagging when it is actually the hinged post leaning in from the weight of the gate.

Strong Gate Posts

You need a post that is securely anchored and of adequate strength and fitness to support the gate. Gate postholes should be dug deeper and generously anchored with concrete. It's fine to use 4 x 4 posts for most gates up to $3^1/2$ feet wide, but gates wider than 4 feet should be hung on 6 x 6 or larger posts. It is a good idea for gates that are wider than 5 feet to be split into two sections.

A double-door gate has one section that is normally opened for foot traffic and a second section that is opened when you need to get large items through, such as your lawn tractor. The second gate that is not routinely opened is usually anchored to the walkway with a ground pin that keeps it stationary while the primary gate door is opened and closed in normal use.

Strong Gate Frames

Keeping your gate strong and firm through temperature extremes and periods of wet and dry weather is the challenge you face when building your gate. These changes in temperature and moisture cause your gate components to expand and contract, pulling and tugging on your fasteners. You need to design a gate that will remain strong.

Z-Frame Gates

One of the simplest, yet strongest methods of building a gate is to use a Z frame. The Z frame gets its name from the three structural members used to support the gate's infill—two horizontal and one diagonal. The bottom of the diagonal member meets the horizontal member near the bottom hinge. That means that the top of the diagonal member extends away from the hinged side of the gate. This design helps to shift more of the gate's weight to the bottom hinge and the bottom of the supporting post. Put in simpler terms, Z frames get their strength from channeling all the downward pressure from the non-hinged side of the gate to the hinged side of the gate. Even a split Z frame, where the diagonal bar of the Z is made from two diagonal members split by a middle gate rail, is still very strong and resistant to sagging.

The diagonal brace of the Z frame can be placed between two rails if the infill is sturdy. In this case the infill acts as the vertical members of the frame. If the infill is too frail to act as reliable vertical support for the size gate you are producing, then a complete perimeter frame should be constructed.

With the perimeter frame, two verticals and two horizontals form the perimeter of the rectangle. A fifth diagonal member is added to give extra strength. It is attached on the bottom hinge side and extends diagonally across the gate to the top of the latched side. As you can tell by its description, the diagonal member

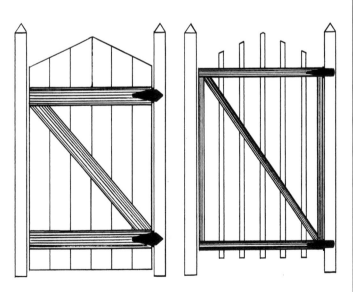

Above: The Z-frame gate can be used when the gate infill is sturdy and capable of supplying the vertical support to the gate. The perimeter frame gate can be used when the gate infill is frail, because it does not require the infill for its vertical support. Right: A selection of Z-frame gates.

forms a Z in the perimeter frame and helps to provide the same type of support as in the basic Z frame. A perimeter frame will allow you to apply your infill to a frame without relying on the infill for vertical support of your gate.

Halflap, rabbet, dado, and basic butt joints can be used when making the perimeter of the gate. Though butt joints are the easiest to construct, they offer the least structural support. If you use the butt joint, you can add L mending plates for a stronger connection.

The reverse Z frame is also used to channel weight from the non-hinged side of the gate to the hinged side. In the case of the reverse Z, rather than working by using the compressing forces of the weight of the gate, it uses pulling power to transfer the weight to the top of the hinged post.

X-Frame Gates

Your gate can have the strength of both the Z and the reverse Z by employing both in one gate: the X frame. Often gate designers will use these X frames just for the symmetry in appearance; however, the extra strength provided by the X frame is certainly no harm to the homeowner who wants a trouble-free gate that transfers its weight effectively to the hinged gate post.

Above and right: A selection of X-frame gates.

Other Gate Supports

Sometimes when you design a gate, you don't want a visible Z or X. If you understand the function of the diagonal supports in frame design, you will be able to modify the Z to produce a gate that matches your fence's visual appearance while maintaining a good level of strength. One way to do this is by using diagonally placed infill. The diagonal infill does the same job as the Z bar, transferring all the weight of the gate to the hinged side.

Still another more subtle method is to reduce the size of the diagonal bracing enough that it no longer looks like a Z in your gate. This reduced diagonal bracing will still help transfer weight from the gate to the hinged post. Of course the more it is reduced in size, the less support the diagonal bracing will provide.

If you want to avoid diagonals all together, use good joinery and hardware to create a rigid gate frame. The difficulty here is making a tight frame that will not be weakened or loosened by moisture or temperature changes. There are metal support brackets, usually in the shape of an L, that can be placed in the four corners of the wooden perimeter frame.

Above: Diagonal infill can be used for support and decoration. Right: Blocking between the pickets and sturdy hinges held on with bolts rather than screws keep this gate in good form without the use of diagonal bracing.

This Swiss Chalet has a handsome gate that utilizes large, decorative L-brace hardware held on with heavy-duty lag screws to support the frame, omitting the need for the traditional diagonal bracing.

A less attractive but easy-to-use alternative for gate support is to install a turnbuckle. A turnbuckle, like a Z frame, is installed diagonally and is used to lift the weight of the gate. If the weight of the gate is causing your gate post to lean, a turnbuckle applied from the top of your gate post to the bottom of the adjacent post will help to straighten the gate post and lift the gate.

A final hardware alternative is to use massive, stable hinges that provide enough support to the gate frame's horizontal members that it is virtually impossible for the gate to shift out of square from its own weight. The only way to bend the gate from being square would be to apply enough weight to bend the hinges themselves. Specialty hinges of this strength require a good bit of metal and will have a higher price tag, but they could help significantly in producing a strong gate without a diagonal support.

Making and Attaching Gates

Once you have decided upon your gate's design, size, location, swing direction, and material, it is time to actually begin making the gate. If you are not using a pre-planned gate pattern, you may want to make a scale drawing of your gate and fence. From this drawing you will be able to see how the fence, posts, and gate will look together. You will also be able to calculate the size of each piece of lumber to be used in the gate.

Location and spacing of gate hardware should also be shown on the scale drawing. This will help you evaluate which locations look and function better for hinges and latches.

Now that you have an overall understanding of how gates are constructed and how they function, here is a summary of step-by-step procedures for building a gate.

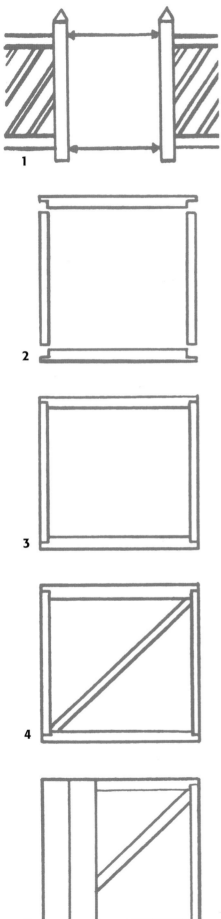

1. **Measure the opening.** Measure at two places, along the top and along the bottom of the area between the post that will hold the hinges and the post that will hold the latch. Your overall gate size should be the distance between your posts, minus the clearance for your hinges and opening swing, usually 1/2 to 1 inch. Clearance is needed to keep the gate from catching on the posts as it swings open. Some hardware may require additional clearance. Hinges mounted on the outer face of the post require little clearance to open and close the gate. Most T and strap hinges fall into this category and are the most commonly used hinges on gates for picket fences. Hinges mounted inside the post, like hook screw and eye hinges or hook screw and strap hinges, will require the extra distance that they protrude from the side of the post as clearance.

2. **Cut the frame parts.** Cut the stock to the necessary lengths, and prepare and cut the joints if you are planning to use special joints. Cut cross members to overlay the upright members in order to keep water from entering the joints.

3. **Assemble the joints.** Assemble the perimeter of the frame into a rectangle. Continually check and adjust to maintain square as you attach the pieces to one another. You can use nails, screws, or bolts to connect the gate perimeter pieces. Bolts or screws will provide a more permanent and secure fit, making your gate stronger and more stable. Once the frame is assembled, you can make a final check for square. Measure both diagonal stretches across the gate; if the measurements are the same, the gate is square.

4. **Add the diagonal bracing.** Lay your diagonal brace and place the frame on top of it. Place 2 x 4 blocks under the unsupported corners to hold the frame level. With a pencil, mark the lines where you will cut the diagonal member. When sawing your diagonal member, do not cut on the line, but cut immediately next to it on the outer side. This will ensure a snug fit. Toe screw the diagonal support in place.

5. **Add the infill**. Lay the frame down so that you can add the infill. Make certain that the diagonal brace bottom will be on the hinge side of the gate.

   Note: Steps 4 and 5 are frequently flipped depending on the gate infill and type specifics. Perimeter frames are usually made in this order, but the diagonal brace of the Z frame is usually applied after all the infill is attached.

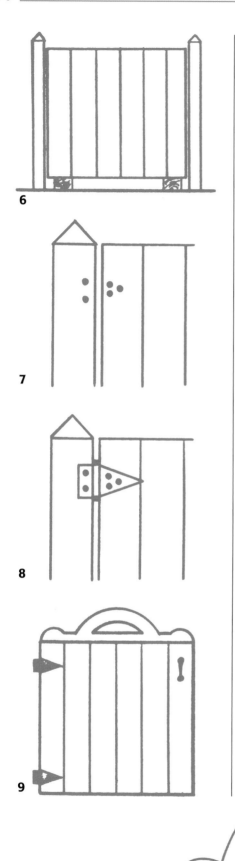

6. Check the fit. Use scrap boards or bricks to prop the gate to its correct height in the gate opening. Use shims to keep desired spacing at posts. Have a helper balance the gate while you check the fit. Take your hinges and gate latch, and mark their locations on the posts and gate.

7. Fasten hinges to gate. Install hinges with the longest screws or bolts that will not poke through the far side of your post and gate lumber. Attach the hinges and latch mechanism on the gate first. Refit the gate to make certain that the post hinge markings match up with the hinges already attached to the gate.

8. Hang the gate. Drill pilot holes in the post for gate hinge screws or bolts. Attach the gate and check its swing for post clearance and maximum opening distance. Mark the latch catch position on the post, and install the latch mechanism onto the post.

Note: Steps 7 and 8 are frequently flipped. If hanging a new gate on a freshly built fence, it is usually easiest to do in this order. When replacing a gate on an existing fence and reusing the hinges and hinge location on the post, the hinges should stay attached or be reattached to the gate in their prior locations. Then the gate should be attached to the hinges.

9. Add detail pieces. Add latches and pulls. Appliqués and pediments are frequently applied after the gate is hung to reduce the chance of damaging the detail work. They also create more flat surfaces on the gate that can be checked for plumb and level during the hanging process.

10. Apply finish. Finish with an appropriate treatment of wood sealer, stain, or paint.

Techniques for Building the Fence You Want

While fences frequently require customization to meet your specific needs, these detailed steps will help you see the progression to building fence infill, decorative posts, and gates.

Where curving cuts are required for these projects, patterns have been included in the patterns section of this book.

Making Full-Bodied Sawn Pickets from a Pattern

Materials and Tools Needed

Lumber: 5/4 x 6 deck boards cut to 36 inches in length for pickets.
Tools: Band saw.

This stunning fence with full-bodied sawn pickets and charming corner posts and gates may appear to be a difficult accomplishment. Beginners are often intimidated by full-bodied sawn pickets. The assumption is that they are too complicated to cut, or will take too long to make. This section will demonstrate not only how to cut out a picket, but also how to make modifications to your pattern and identify efficient ways to cut picket details.

Select or create a pattern for your picket and make a cardboard or hardboard template from it. Transfer your pattern to cardboard or hardboard to make a more durable template. If making many pickets, you may want to go with hardboard templates, which will be more durable and last for a long time. Each picket in this fence was cut from a deck board that measured 1 x 5^{1}/$_{2}$ x 36.

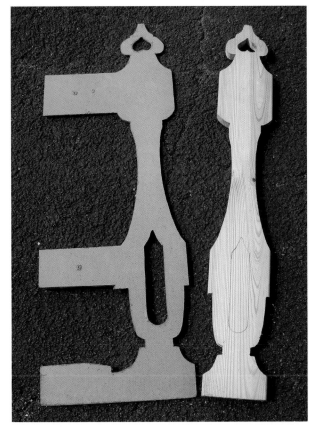

Cut a test picket using your pattern. By doing this, you can determine if you want to eliminate some features. For instance, time balanced with personal taste may have an impact on how you want to proceed. In fact, while I was cutting this picket, I found that it was too much work to make the interior heart and elongated teardrop shown in this picture. It took me as long to cut out the heart as it did to cut the entire outside of the picket. I decided after the test that the interior cuts just did not add enough interest to justify the extra time I would need to spend.

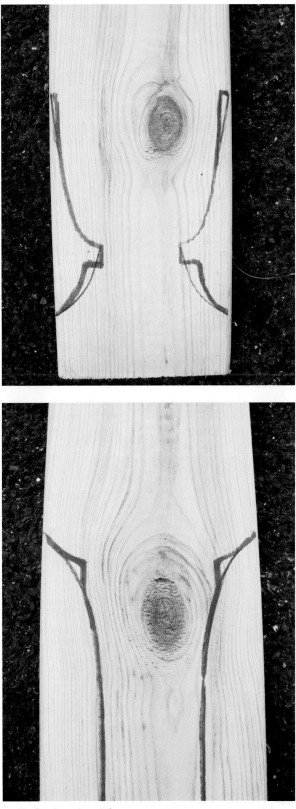

To further simplify your cutting, you may want to reduce the number of lines. The heavy marker line is the outline of the original pattern. The thinner pencil line represents a simplification of that pattern. This would be one way to simplify the base, but it does noticeably change the pattern. I opted to keep these details, as I felt losing them changed the pattern too much.

Adjust the saw guide height for your lumber thickness. When using a band saw, you want to adjust your blade guide to a height 1/4 inch above the height needed for your lumber to pass under the guide. This will allow your guide to provide maximum support to your blade. The lower the guide, the more support it can provide to the blade.

This adjustment height is higher than it should be for the best cut, but for instructional purposes it allows you to see the lumber behind the blade to better understand the cut being made. When you actually cut your pickets, set your guide just 1/4 inch above the height of your lumber as shown in the prior step.

Begin cutting the base according to diagram on page 79. Attempt to cut out this picket using the efficient sequence of cuts we devised in the earlier diagram for cutting the bottom portion of the picket.

Determine if you will alter features. You may find that you don't want to eliminate some details of your pattern, but you do want to simplify them or modify them in a way that makes the pattern easier to cut. I found a few spots that slowed me down while cutting the outside edge of the picket. The most difficult for me with my particular band saw and blade size was cutting this notch at the base of the baluster. It was a tight space for me to make these sharp corners. It took a good bit of time to chip the corners out. Following are some ways to avoid making these two 90-degree angles in the base.

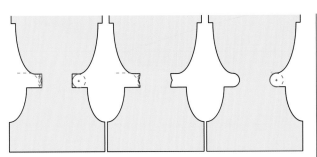

Change the shape of the lines. This diagram shows two barely noticeable methods for changing the problem area of the pattern. The first actually adds a small detail, a nib. Cutting this nib in two passes will be easy using a band saw. The second uses a drill press to make a round cut in the base. This would be very easy to do, but you would need to change tools from the band saw to the drill press. Changing tools will add time and effort. Since we don't need the drill press for any other cuts on this picket, it will be more efficient to add the nib and cut the entire picket using only the band saw.

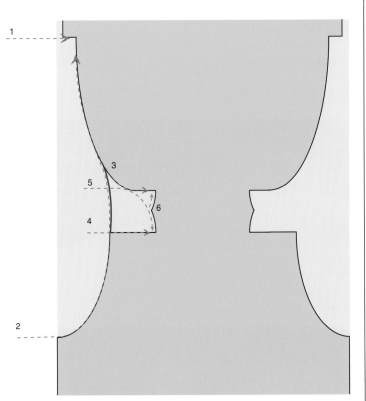

Examine for the most efficient approach. There is always more than one way to cut a picket. While the band saw is a fun tool to use, you do not want to make unnecessary cuts or spend more time turning off your saw and backing out of cuts. This diagram demonstrates an efficient way to cut out the details in the base of this picket. As you cut, refer to the diagram along with the step-by-step instructions and photographs on the ensuing pages.

Make cut 1. This cut is so shallow that you can probably make it without turning off your saw to back out of the cut.

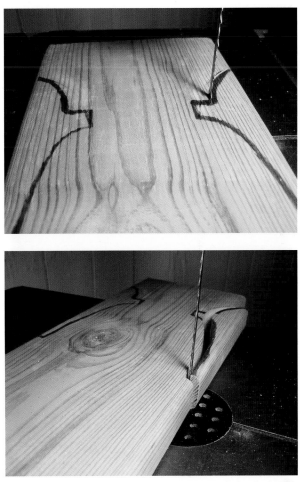

Make cut 2. Start from the bottom of the baluster pedestal. Continue though the cut all the way to join up with cut 1. The scrap piece will fall away.

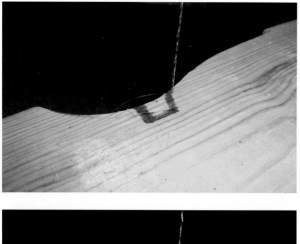

Align the picket to begin making cut 3 along the base of the rounded bowl of the baluster. Make the cut, turn off the saw, and back the picket out of the blade.

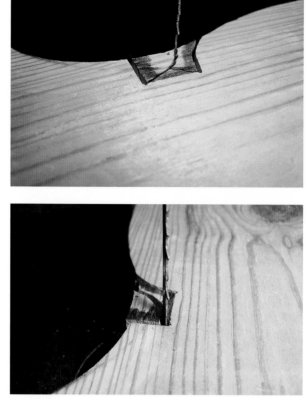

The arcs for cuts 5 and 6 are drawn here in pencil. Align the picket to begin making cut 5. Make the cut and the scrap piece will fall away.

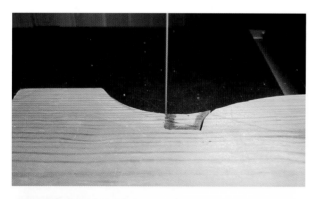

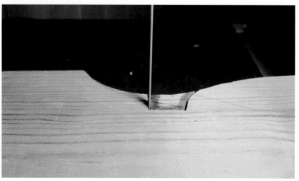

Align the picket to begin making cut 4 at the top of the baluster pedestal. As in the prior step, make the cut, turn off the saw, and back the picket out of the blade.

Finally, align the picket to begin making cut 6. Make the cut and the tiny scrap piece will fall away.

Now you are ready to cut picket body side.

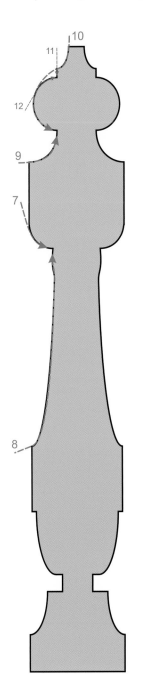

Determine the most efficient approach for the rest of the picket side. The base—the most complicated part to cut on this picket—was done in six cutting steps. Now examine the picket body cuts. By making the short cut (No. 7) before making the much longer cut (No. 8), you will be able to reduce the distance you must back the blade out of the picket. Finally, examine the picket top. Again, making the shorter cut (No. 9) before making the longer cut (No. 10) will reduce the distance you must back the blade out of the picket. Finally, cuts 11 and 12 are both very short, removing just a small bit of wood; however, they are essential to give this picket top definition.

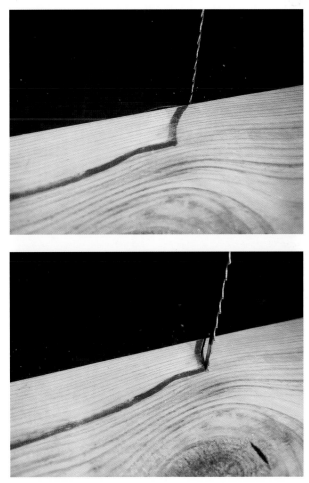

Next, you will work your way up one side of the picket and down the other until all the cutouts are done. Begin by aligning the picket for the seventh cut. Make the cut, turn off the saw, and back the picket out of the blade. Next, align the picket for the next cut. Make the cut; the scrap piece will fall away.

Align the picket to cut the base of the picket top. Attempting to do this on this saw using this pattern with the thickness and distance of this band saw's throat, I can almost line up the cut, but my band saw throat is in the way. I will not be able to make the cut and stay on the line. I could trace this part of the picket top on the back of the picket and cut it out from the back, or I can first cut the other side of the picket body before cutting the top and have enough room at the throat to start the cut.

Cut the opposite side of the picket body. Once again, align the picket to cut the base of the picket top. Now, with both sides of the picket body cut away, I have a finger's width to spare. I will be able to make this cut without needing to trace part of the picket pattern on the back.

Begin cutting the picket top. Cut to the base of the picket top, turn off the saw, and back the picket out of the blade. This completes cut 9.

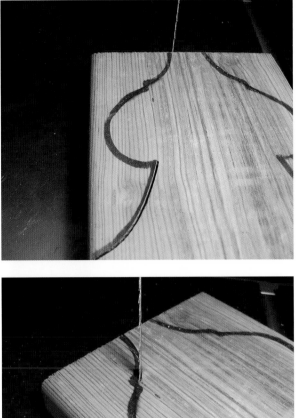

Cut to the picket top. Cut the inside of the line, leaving the excess marker on the scrap pieces that fall away from the picket. Note that when you reach the top of the nib, you will be on the outside of the line.

Slowly work back to the inside of the line and continue cutting out the picket top. Continue through the cut all the way to join up with the cut you made previously, completing cut 10. The scrap piece will fall away. Cut out both sides of the picket top this way.

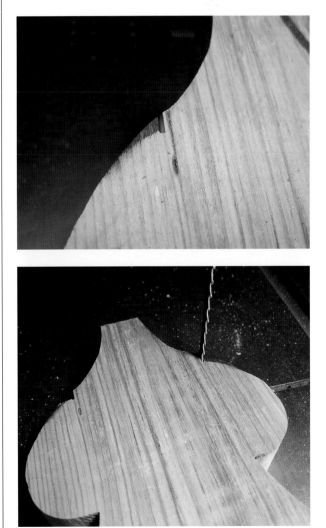

You will need to make two very small cuts (nos. 11 and 12) on each side to the picket tops to form the nibs.

The picket bodies remained unchanged.

Compare the test picket to the final picket. After making a few changes to this picket design we were able to reduce the amount of time it takes to cut out each picket.

The picket tops were simplified back to the original pattern without the addition of cutouts.

The picket bottoms were modified to make them easier to cut by adding a small nib to the detail of the picket bottom.

Easy Finials for Post Tops

Materials and Tools Needed

Lumber: Wood block cut from 5 x 5 post.
Tools: Band saw with 3/8-inch blade.

This is a beautiful urn finial that is easier to make than many designs, because it has few lines and the curves flow gently. I suggest you use a 3/8-inch band saw blade to allow you to more easily make the turns in the pattern. Use a good quality block that is not twisted or severely checked or cracked. You need flat sides against the band saw table to accurately cut the finial.

Number the pieces that you are going to cut away. Place the block so that you can see both adjacent sides with the traced pattern. Number the corners. The outer corner of the left side is 1, the outer corner of the right side is 2, the inner corner of the left side is 3, and the inner corner of the right side is 4.

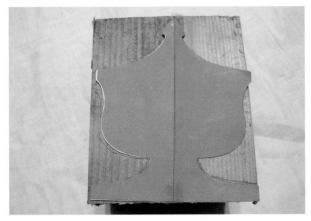

Select the paper pattern of the appropriate size for your block of wood. This block was cut from a 4 1/2-inch-square post so I selected a 4 1/2-inch-wide finial pattern. Trace the pattern on two adjacent sides of the block. Be careful to make sure you position the pattern accurately so that the urn base and cup lip touch precisely.

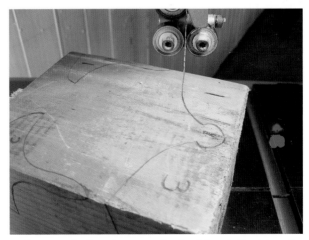

Start with the pieces marked with a 1. Position the block as pictured.

Begin by cutting the upper slope.

Cut to the base of the acorn finial and stop; turn the saw off and back the blade out of the block of wood.

Reposition the block so that you can begin cutting the top slope of the acorn finial.

Cut the top slope of the finial and stop when the cut is too tight for you to stay on your line. Turn off the band saw and back out of the cut

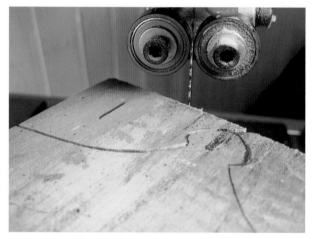

Position the block so that you can cut the lower slope of the acorn finial. You will cut through the block until you can meet up with your pencil line.

Cut through the block until the piece falls away from the block of wood.

Next you will cut away the lower piece marked 1. Position the block as pictured.

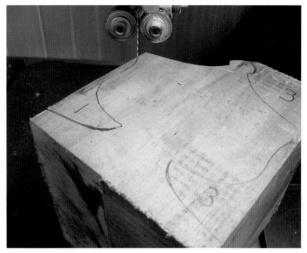

Reposition the block so that you can begin cutting the side of the urn bowl.

Begin cutting away the upper slope.

Cut through the block until the piece falls away from the block of wood.

Cut to the base of the urn bowl and stop. Turn the saw off and back the blade out of the block of wood.

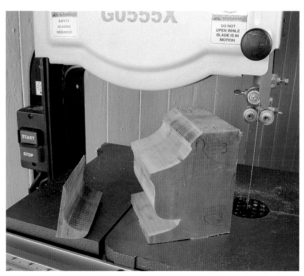

If you set this finial on its base, this is what it will look like at this point.

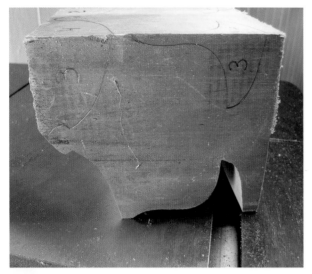

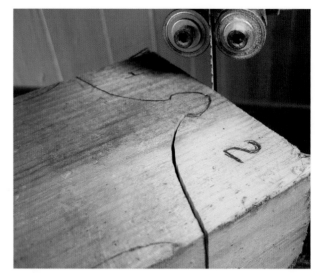

If you set the finial on the side you just cut, you will notice that there are two points of contact—at the base of the urn and at the lip of the urn bowl—that were not cut. Because there are two points of contact that are uncut, the finial will remain flat on the table while we cut out the edge marked with a 2.

Reposition the block so that you can begin cutting the top slope of the acorn finial as you did previously. Cut the finial's top slope and stop when the cut is too tight for you to stay on your line. Turn off the band saw and back out of the cut. Position the block so that you can cut the lower slope of the acorn finial. You will cut through the block until you can meet up with your pencil line. Cut through the block until the piece falls away from the block of wood.

Now you will move on to the pieces marked 2. You will follow the same steps as you did to cut out the pieces marked with a 1. Again, cut the top slope of the urn. Cut to the base of the acorn finial and stop. Turn the saw off and back the blade out of the block of wood.

Next you will cut away the lower piece marked 2. Position the block as pictured. Begin by cutting the pedestal slope of the urn.

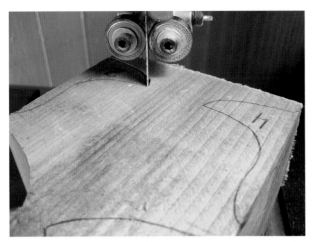

Cut to the base of the urn bowl and stop. Turn the saw off and back the blade out of the block of wood.

Reposition the block so that you can begin cutting the side of the urn bowl. Cut through the block until the piece falls away from the block of wood.

If you set this urn on its base, this is what it will look like at this point. All the pieces numbered 1 and 2 are cut away.

You will now begin to cut the pieces marked 3, but take note that you should not cut them off completely. If you do, you will not have any pencil marks to follow on side 4. Position the block as pictured and begin cutting the pedestal slope of the urn.

Cut away the pedestal slope until you are 1/2 inch from the base of the urn bowl and stop. Remember: Do not cut the wood all the way to the base. Turn the saw off and back the blade out of the block of wood.

Reposition the block so that you can begin cutting the side of the urn bowl.

Cut through the block until you reach the base of the urn bowl. The piece will not fall away this time because you did not complete the cut of the line in the previous step.

Next cut away the lower piece marked 4.

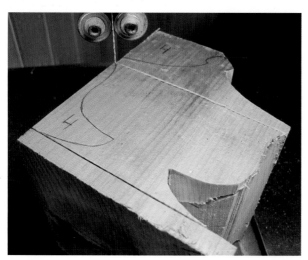

Position the block as pictured. Begin by cutting the urn bowl.

Cut to the base of the urn bowl where it meets the pedestal and stop, turn the saw off, and back the blade out of the block of wood.

Reposition the block so that you can begin cutting the slope of the pedestal.

Cut through the block until the piece falls away from the block of wood. Turn the finial so that side 3 is face up.

Notice that the portion with the pencil markings fell away after you completed the cut on 4.

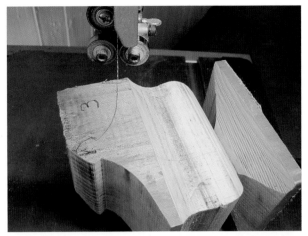

Position the block as pictured. Begin cutting the top slope of the urn.

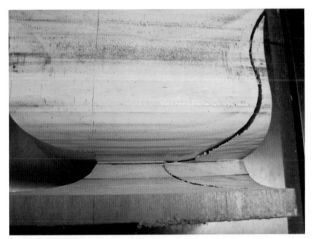

Take a pencil and sketch in the completion of the cut on the contour on the pedestal. Use the band saw and cut the sketched line.

Begin cutting away the upper slope. Cut to the base of the acorn finial and stop. Turn the saw off and back the blade out of the block of wood.

The pedestal is now completely cut out. Turn the finial so that the side marked 3 is face up.

Reposition the block so that you can begin cutting the top slope of the acorn finial.

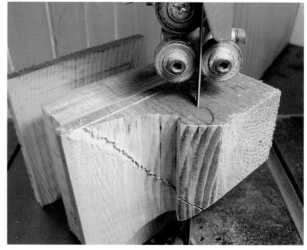

Cut to the base of the acorn finial and stop. Turn the saw off and back the blade out of the block of wood.

Cut the acorn finial's top slope. Stop when the cut begins to turn under the finial. Turn off the band saw and back out of the cut.

Reposition the block so that you can begin cutting the top slope of the acorn finial.

Turn the finial so that side 4 is face up. Position the block as pictured. Begin by cutting the top slope of the urn.

Cut the acorn finial's top slope. Stop when the cut is too tight for you to stay on your line. Turn off the band saw and back out of the cut.

Position the block so that you can cut the lower slope of the acorn finial. You will cut through the block until you can meet up with your pencil line.

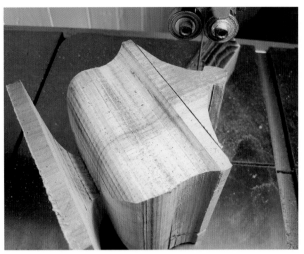

Cut through the block until the piece falls away from the block of wood. Turn the finial so that side 3 is face up.

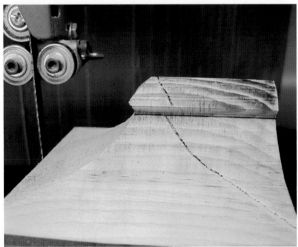

Notice that the portion with the pencil markings fell away after you completed the cut on 4.

Take a pencil and sketch in the completion of the cut on the contour on the pedestal.

Cut out the sketched line using the band saw.

Here is the finial cut out entirely.

Here are three more examples of post caps topped with finials cut using this square turning method. These are slightly more complex to cut because they involve more lines, which means more stops and starts, but the same basic process applies.

Modifying a Fence with Molding: The Layered Look

Materials and Tools Needed

Lumber: 2 x 4 for pickets and rails, 1 x 3 furring boards, cellular PVC shingle molding, cellular PVC lattice molding.
Tools: Band saw, hand drill.

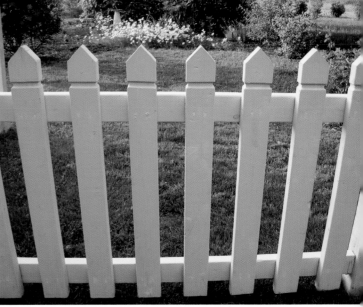

You may already own a sturdy, functional fence. Here are some techniques to spice up a nice but boring fence. They demonstrate how you can build upon your simple picket fence. By removing wood from the picket and adding layers using molding, this charming fence obtains interesting depth and shadowing. This example uses two shades of green to accent the fence, but you should substitute the trim colors from your house to tie your entire property together visually.

There is one more modification I would suggest to anyone making this fence completely from scratch. Cut the angle of the pointed tops to match the angle of the roofline of your own home or another prominent building on the property. This is a subtle way to match the fence to existing structures on the site, giving a pleasing visual effect.

Assuming you are starting with a simple white fence made of 2 x 4 pickets and rails that you want to give a bit more pizzazz, you might try a birdhouse picket design, with molding that adds a layered look.

Note the grooved neck of the picket tops. A router mounted in a router table was used to create this effect when the pickets were initially cut. If you are willing to disassemble the pickets on your fence, you can use a table saw with a crosscut sled to make the grooves. Otherwise, you can just paint a straight line across the picket top to represent the bottom of the birdhouse.

Use a paint pad to paint the birdhouse pale green above the groove. I find using a paint pad much easier than using a brush or roller for small surfaces.

Again, use a paint pad to paint the roof of the birdhouse picket. A great way to tie your fence to the rest of the property is to use the same color as the roofs of the buildings on the property.

Find a good location for the door. Here, I measured 3 3/4 inches down from the center peak of the picket to find the center. Use a 1-inch Forstner bit to make the door. Drill until the bit is 3/4 inch into the wood.

The result will look like this.

Use sanding bits to quickly and efficiently get rid of burrs and rough spots in the holes.

Prime and then paint the birdhouse door using the same color used to paint your roof.

Choose your appliqué materials. Appliqués can be large or small. I like to make small or thin appliqués from synthetic materials, because synthetics will not crack and split as readily as wood. Larger appliqués are less likely to crack and split, so synthetic may not be worth the extra cost to you. Thin wood lattice will split and crack over the seasons; however, this synthetic cellular PVC lattice will last for decades. I also find it easier to pre-paint my smaller moldings and appliqués and just touch them up at the cut marks.

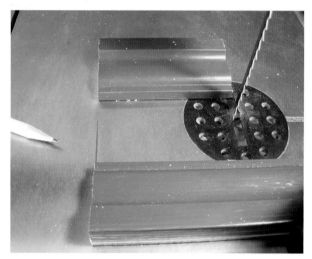

Next, cut the collar moldings for all the pickets to the correct length using a band saw. Since the pickets are 3½ inches wide, the shingle moldings will be cut to 3½ inches in length. Use a pencil mark on your band saw table to help you see how long to cut each piece of shingle molding as you run it through the blade, using the miter guide with a 0-degree angle adjustment (or no angle adjustment).

Now, cut the necktie molding to length. Again, use a mark on the band saw table to guide you on how long to cut each piece of lattice molding. Use the miter guide to cut the lattice to length.

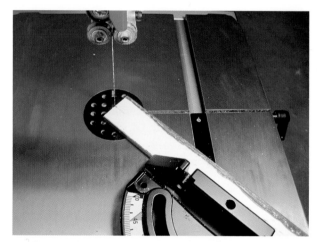

Flip the lattice to see the back and use a pencil to mark its center.

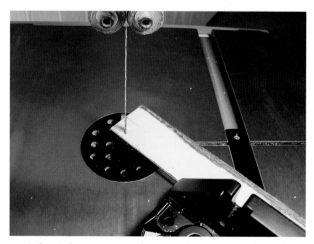

Adjust the miter guide to a 45-degree angle and cut one side of the point of the necktie.

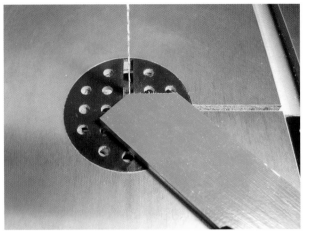

Flip the lattice again to see the front and cut the other side of the point of the necktie.

When you are done cutting the neckties, you may find minor differences in length. Do not worry about differences that are less that 1/4 inch, because they will be barely noticeable.

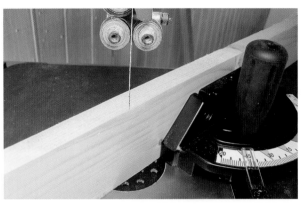

Next, you will make the base boots. Unlike the collar, which extends all the way from one edge of the picket to the other, the base boot is narrower and shows a little of the picket all around it. This base boot is 8 inches high and 2½ inches wide, with a 45-degree angle at the top. To cut the top of the base boot, use a band saw with the miter guide adjusted to a 45-degree angle.

Cut the bottom of the base boot using the band saw with the miter guide set to a 0-degree angle adjustment.

Now you will apply the appliqués. Mark two lines across your pickets with chalk to align your collar and base boot. Mark one line 4 inches below the bottom of the groove of the birdhouse picket. Mark another line 1½ inches above the bottom of the pickets.

Attach the collar shingle molding flush with the chalk mark using rust-resistant finishing nails.

Attach the necktie lattice molding visually centered on the picket and butted up against the collar.

Center the base boot on the picket and attach it. Continue on to the next picket, attaching the collar, necktie, and boot.

Here is the completed fence.

Modifying a Fence with Paint:
The Illusion of Depth and Design Stamps

Materials and Tools Needed

Existing plain fence, paint, and painting tools.

You can use paint to add design and also create an illusion of layering to make an existing simple picket fence appear to be more ornate than it truly is. The effect of a full-bodied sculpted picket is achieved by using dark-colored paint on the edges of the picket to give the illusion a portion of the picket is cut away. In the light of the afternoon sun, it's obvious the pickets are painted, but in the dim light of dusk the illusion is more effective.

You can also buy or make your own stamps to decorate each picket with a repeating design. The fleur-de-lis design on the fence above was made from a stamp I created from craft foam and cut out with an X-Acto knife. Paint pad refills cut to shape and attached to a

foam or wood block can also make good stamps. I find that paint pads hold more paint and apply it more evenly than craft foam.

Again, I would recommend changing the angle of the pointed tops to match the angle of the roofline of your own house or other prominent building on the property. By tying the fence to existing structures on the site, you will achieve a balance that is aesthetically pleasing.

Start with an ordinary white picket fence. In this example, we will use shades of green paint, but you can choose shades of any color to better match your house. Use a paint pad to paint the picket sides a pale green. Clean the pad and then use it to paint the rooftop of the picket with the dark green.

Begin stamping; try to visually center each stamp and apply even pressure. You may want to measure and mark the location for accuracy, or you may want to take a chance and do it freehand. If you want a homemade look, don't worry about minor smudges or blots (like the one on the picket that is closest to us in this picture). Minor differences between pickets will make your fence look hand done, which it is, and not mass printed.

Prepare the stamp for adding the design to the tops of your pickets.

To create the picket body sculpting, use a paint pad on a stick to darken the left and right sides of the front of the picket. I like to use one side of a paint pad corner. Pick a location to start your sculpted painting. I start two fingers width below the fleur-de-lis. Apply steady, even pressure as you drag to your stopping point near the bottom of the picket.

Here is the completed section of the tri-color painted picket fence in early evening light, when the illusion of depth is most effective.

Inset Infill: Lattice Fence with Quatrefoil Designs

Materials and Tools Needed

Lumber: 2 x 4 synthetic lumber for rails
1 x 4 synthetic lumber for stiles
1 x 6 synthetic lumber for infill
4 x 4 synthetic lumber for posts
(I used BJM Industries lumber for this project)

2¹/₂-inch or longer screws.

Tools: Table saw (you can substitute a miter saw because there are no rip cuts required), hand drill with hole saw bit, speed square, spade shovel, clamshell posthole digger, metal auger bar, two spirit levels, hammer.

This fence design uses an oversized lattice made from 1 x 6 boards to achieve a much bolder look than the more commonly found finer and thinner lattices. Beautiful and relatively simple in appearance and construction, this is still a grid fence with the infill inset to the frame.

Even simple inset infills require more precision in cutting and assembling than mounted infills. Insets are also less forgiving with minor changes in distance between posts.

The dimensions given in this fence are to be used as a guide and not gospel. Variations in lumber sizes will impact the actual dimensions of your fence panel. For example, the 1 x 6 lumber used to make the lattice slats were exactly 5¹/₂ inches wide. Although that is exactly the expected width for 1 x 6s, it is not uncommon for them to vary by up to an ¹/₈ inch. If my 1 x 6s had been 5⁷/₁₆ inches wide, the final dimensions of the fence panel would have been smaller. When making a grid design, it is a good idea to cut and assemble one complete panel before cutting the infill and frame members for all panels. This will allow you to determine and notate any modifications to measurements to fit your true lumber sizes.

The central cutout design in this fence is called a quatrefoil, which means "four leaves." The quatrefoil was used by the medieval Moors in their designs, and its use can be seen throughout the Mediterranean, especially in Spain. From Spain, the quatrefoil design traveled to the New World and was used in Mexican, Texan, and Californian architecture.

First, you will create the rectangular frame. For this particular fence, each section measures 87 5/8 inches in length by 34 1/8 inches in height on the outside of the frame. However, the interior rectangle of your frame will need to measure 86 1/8 by 31 1/8 inches to accommodate your infill. The top and bottom rails are made of 2 x 4s, the end stiles are made from 1 x 4s. Cut your 2 x 4 rails to 86 1/8 inches in length. Cut your 1 x 4 stiles to 34 1/8 inches in length.

You now lay out the 1 x 4s to lift your infill. You do not want to attach the infill flush with the down side of the frame. You want to raise the infill about 3/4 inch so that it will be inset 3/4 inch. Do that by laying two long 1 x 4s inside the frame that are almost as long as the rails. Then lay two shorter scraps of 1 x 4s in the middle of each style. You will not attach these to the frame; they are only there to raise the infill while you attach it.

Assemble your frame on a large flat area like a driveway or patio. Attach your stiles overlapping the ends of the rails. This should give you the needed interior dimensions of 86 1/8 by 31 1/8 inches for your infill.

Using 1 x 6 stock, cut eight parallelograms. For each, you will trim off the end of your 1 x 6. Then, from your fresh 45-degree cut, measure 44 inches. Mark your 1 x 6 and cut it to make a parallelogram that measures 44 inches on the long side and 7 3/4 inches on the short side.

While keeping your frame square, lay out all your parallelograms in the frame. You should be able to lay out seven parallelograms with the points of the first and last pieces resting in the corner of the frame. What if the parallelograms don't fit exactly? If it is just a minimal amount off, such as 1/4 inch short, you may just want to trim the corner off your last full-sized parallelogram. If the variation is greater, you should disassemble the frame and trim the rails or cut new rails to fit the exact distance. Note this so that you cut your next set of rails to this modified length.

Use a speed square to make sure you keep the infill at a 45-degree angle while you attach it. Do not attach the second parallelogram; it is only there as a spacer to keep 5 1/2 inches between the first and third parallelograms. Now attach the third, fifth, and seventh parallelograms.

Remove the spacer parallelograms. Here is what the frame should look like at this point.

Now, attach the first parallelogram using four 2 1/2-inch or longer screws, two on each rail. It doesn't matter which end you start with, because both the top and bottom of the infill are identical.

The completed fence section has four medium-length boards and four triangle boards, two of each used on the ends of the section.

For the triangles, you want to cut them so the long side of the triangle measures 11 inches.

For the medium-length boards, each end will be cut at a 45-degree angle; however, the angles will not be parallel to each other as they were in the long pieces that make up the bulk of the infill. The longest side of the medium-length board will measure 32⅝ inches; the opposite side will measure 21⅝ inches, provided your 1 x 6 board is exactly 5½ inches wide.

Place one of the triangles in the upper corner against the top rail. Use an extra scrap of 1 x 6 as a spacer and lay out a medium length board. Attach both the triangle and medium-length board to the top rail and the side stile using two screws in each end. Repeat these instructions for the opposite bottom corner.

Lay out the next layer on top of your completed first layer in the opposite direction and attach. Use extra 1 x 6 boards as spacers to get the layout spaced properly. You may need blocks to hold up the triangle corners and prevent them from tipping. Attach your infill using four screws per board.

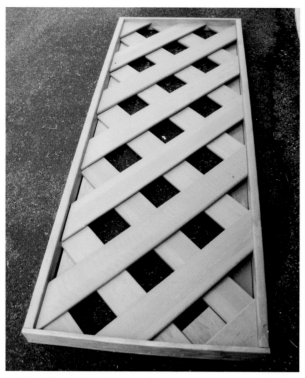

The fence should now look like this. If you want a simple lattice style, you can stop at this point. The remainder of this section will give directions for the quatrefoil windows in the center row of the lattice.

Use a 2-inch-diameter hole-cutting attachment for your drill to cut semicircles out of the sides of the square windows to make them quatrefoil windows. The 1/8-inch holes you drilled in the prior step will help guild the pilot bit of the hole saw bit so that you do not slip off the edge of your 1 x 6 board.

On the upper layer of the lattice, mark the center of the opposite sides of the window about 1/4 inch in from the edge of the board. Drill small pilot holes using a 1/8-inch bit at your marks. You will want to place a scrap 1x board below your lattice window to provide resistance as you drill.

Use a screwdriver to remove the semicircles from the hole saw bit. You may be able to get a few cuts without cleaning it out after each use, but it is much easier if done after each cut.

Flip the lattice panel over to the opposite side. Repeat the steps you followed for the prior side. Mark, pilot drill, and cut out the semicircles.

You have completed the first panel and are ready to hang it between two posts.

For instructions on how to make the encased decorative post featured with this fence, see page 151.

Installation

Most picket fences are forgiving of small changes in length. Some fences, however, require greater precision in construction and assembling the infill than others. The quatrefoil lattice is one of those fences. Trimming a few inches off a fence section would make it seem visually out of balance. So setting the posts to accommodate the exact length of the infill frame is important.

Start by marking the postholes. If you are making several holes in a row, follow the guidelines on page 47 using strings and a plumb bob to find and mark the location to dig each hole. Then use a pin or paint an X to mark the center of each hole.

Use a spade shovel to dig the first posthole. You want to dig three feet deep, or deep enough for typical fence construction in your area.

As you dig, you will find that you cannot keep the dirt on your shovel as you lift it out of the hole. It is time to move on to a clamshell digger. The clamshell digger works by pinching the dirt in its jaws as you separate the handles

The deeper you go, the harder it gets to dig. Sometimes rocks, or just hard packed dirt, cannot be broken through using a clamshell digger. A heavy solid metal pole auger will usually knock loose big rocks and break up dirt. Posthole augers often have a pointed end for breaking soil and rocks apart and a rounded flat end for tamping dirt back into the posthole when it comes time to set the posts.

Use the post-setting method that you feel is most appropriate for your area, post material, and post use. This fence was made with 100 percent recycled HDPE lumber for all the fence components, including the posts. All the posts were set 3 feet deep using earth and stones to anchor the posts with the exception of the gate posts. For the gate posts, use concrete to securely anchor the posts from the moving forces of the gate. It's a good idea to have help to set your posts. One person can keep the post plumb and aligned squarely with the fence row while the other person incrementally adds and tamps the fill material.

You can also use a bulb-planting bit in your power drill to break up the deeper compacted clay when digging just a few postholes. If you have many to dig, you may want to look into renting a power auger or paying someone with an auger to do it for you.

The encased terminal post is set with its customized side facing the first-run post. This custom side with exposed core post will receive the kickboard and lattice panel in a later step.

Cut the kickboards to the same length as the fence infill. It's much easier to keep the kickboard in place as you check the distance between the two posts and make any needed adjustments to their spacing than it is to use the big lattice fence section. Here is a case where using a kickboard not only adds to the appearance, but is also easier to install. Add and tamp the fill in slow increments while a helper holds the post plumb and in place.

Measure and set the run post in the next posthole. Attach a cleat at 3 feet above the bottom of the post to be parallel to the cleat on the encased post. Then place a backer block of 7 inches in length and 2 inches in width on the run post to mirror the backer block on the encased post. This will be used to support the kickboard and the frame in later steps. Set the run post with just enough dirt and stones to hold the post upright.

Attach the lower kickboard to the run post by toe screwing the 2 x 4 to the post.

Set the upper 2 x 4 kickboard in place. Notice the encased post cradles the 2 x 4s in place. Using screws on this end to secure the kickboard is optional.

Fill the hole in completely, adding dirt and tamping until the post hole is filled and the post is stable and secure.

Attach the upper kickboard to the run post by toe screwing the 2 x 4 to the post as you did for the lower kickboard.

Slide the infill panel into place. This should be easy and the fit should be exact if your panel is as long as your kickboard.

Screw the panel to the run post and the encased post, going through the stiles of the panel frame.

Cut a bevel molding to fit between the two posts and attach it in the center of the rail with finishing nails.

Here is the installed infill. The terminal post and fence are ready to be capped and trimmed with detail pieces.

Here is the completed fence section, installed with kickboard and decorative end post.

Three Picket Styles in One Fence

Materials and Tools Needed

Lumber: Composite clad 4 x 4 posts, composite stockade pickets (3$^{1}/_{2}$ inches wide), composite dog-eared pickets (7 inches wide). I used Fiberon lumber.
Tools: Table saw, band saw, hand drill.

This design takes three easy-to-cut pickets and combines them to make a beautiful picket fence that is simpler in construction than it appears. I was inspired by the Ladyfinger Pickets design on page 169. I liked the general appearance of the design but wanted to reduce the number of appliqué pieces used in the original. I also wanted to make the fence seem lighter, with more visibility through the pickets. The original design used four appliqués on the picket; this design uses one. It also adds a small, thin dagger picket between the sheathed sword pickets to add variety to the infill.

You will need pickets with pointed tops of 3$^{1}/_{2}$ inches wide by 6 feet long to make the swords and daggers. Cut each picket into two pieces, one 40$^{1}/_{2}$ inches long and the other 31$^{1}/_{2}$ inches long. The longer piece will become the sword and the shorter will become the dagger. With the size and height of the guide on my table saw I can safely cut three pickets to length at a time. Your table saw's guide probably has differences from mine. Cut your pickets to length with safety as your first priority and efficiency as your second.

The sword sheath pickets are cut dog-eared fence boards 7 inches wide by 6 feet long. Each finished sheath will be 42 inches in length, so cut the dog-eared fence boards to that length.

Make a copy of the sword handle pattern from the Patterns sections on page 195. Cut out the pattern and center it on the end of the picket. Mark your pattern on the picket with a pencil or a marker. Use a pencil if possible; it produces a thinner line that aids in making more accurate cuts. But if you cannot adequately see a pencil line, use a marker. Marker lines tend to bleed and be thicker.

Use a band saw to cut the sword handle. Cut out as much of the handle as you are able to. Most likely, the throat of the band saw will be in the way and prevent you from making some of the cuts. Skip cutting those lines for now and just cut the lines you are able to without hitting the band saw throat.

Flip over your picket. Take your template and align it with the cuts you were able to make on the other side. Trace the lines you were unable to cut onto the back. Complete cutting out the handle.

Note: Use the same pattern for the handles of the daggers. The only difference between the sword and the dagger is the picket length.

For the blade of the dagger, use a sword blade as a template and trace its profile onto the dagger picket and cut it out.

Make a copy of the sword sheath pattern on page 195. Cut out the pattern and center it on the end of the picket. Cut out your picket on the band saw, except for those lines where the band saw throat prevents you from making the cut.

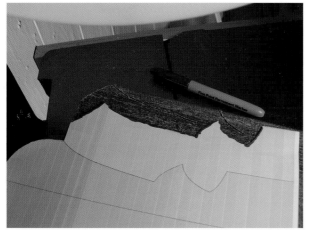

Flip over your picket. Take your template and align it with the cuts you were able to make on the other side.

Trace the lines you were unable to cut onto the back. Complete cutting out the sheath picket.

To make a gable post top, measure 73 1/2 inches from the base of the post and mark it with a line. Adjust your table saw to a 45-degree angle and cut a gabled peak on the post by cutting two opposite sides of the post at a 45-degree angle.

The manufacturer Fiberon makes posts covered with post sleeves of their composite materials that match their fence boards. Here I am using one of these sleeves to make gable roofs for my posts. My posts will be gray, so I am using a reddish post sleeve for contrast with the post roof. Set the table saw at a 45-degree angle and adjust the blade height very low, just high enough to cut through the post sleeve corner. Adjust the table saw's fence to allow you to cut though the corner of the post sleeve. Cut two opposite corners of the post sleeve, turning it into two L-shaped channels.

Take one of the L-shaped channels and cut it into 6-inch-long sections. Each section will become a gabled roof top with about 1-inch overhanging gables on the 4-inch-square posts.

Wait to apply the post caps until after the posts have been set. It will be much easier to set the posts and check them for level without the post caps attached. Use exterior-grade finishing nails or screws to attach the post cap to the post top.

Note: If you do not want to use a post sleeve to make a one-piece gable roof, you could make a two-piece gable roof using extra fence boards cut to rectangles and attached separately to each side of the post-top angle.

When you erect a picket fence using mortised posts to attach rails, the fit between the posts and rails almost always requires that you insert the rails into the mortised slots as you set the posts. This adds a level of complexity to setting the posts compared with other methods where the rails are usually attached after the posts are set. What's more, if the rails already have the pickets attached, it makes the setting of the posts even more cumbersome. For that reason, I find it easier to set the post with just the rails in place and attach the pickets later.

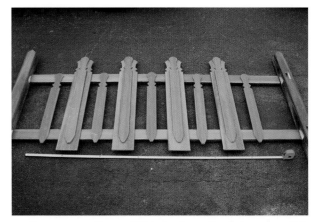

Cut your rails to 83½ inches. To determine this length, I laid out my pattern symmetrically on the rails and determined that the distance between my end pickets, the two end daggers, is 73½ inches. I then allowed for 5 inches on either side of the end dagger, with 1½ inches of that inserted in each post. I used a picket placement with five 3½-inch-wide picket daggers and four 7-inch-wide sheathed sword pickets, all spaced 3½ inches from each other.

For this fence, I set the posts and rails using the manufacturer's instructions. See page 44 for more information on post footing choices.

Attach the first dagger picket 3$^1/_2$ inches away from the post. The dagger picket top should be flush with the rail. Next attach a sheath picket with a sword picket centered on top. You will want to tack swords to the sheaths the prior day with contact cement to make them easier to handle as one unit. You can use an extra picket as a spacer board to get the 3$^1/_2$-inch spacing between the pickets. I also predrilled a hole in the sword at 12 inches from the top of the handle. This allowed me to easily screw the pickets centered on the rail.

Attach the sheathed sword picket with the lowest cut to the gray picket, one finger's width above the top rail.

Here is the completed sword and dagger fence.

Here are some other options for arranging the sword and dagger pickets. The designs would make great privacy fences.

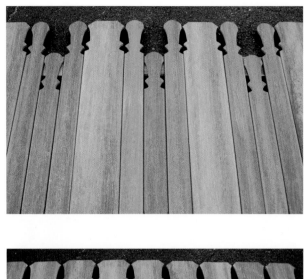

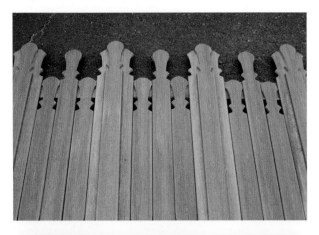

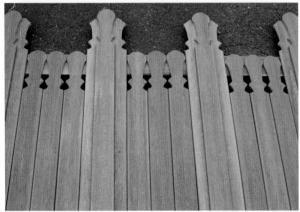

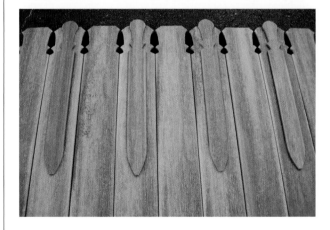

As the sunlight position and intensity changes, so does the look of this fence. By making this fence with layers, you can take greater advantage of the beauty of shadows.

By making the fence with both a cooler gray and a warmer reddish brown, you take greater advantage of the sun's morning and evening red rays. The swords almost glow against the gray sheaths in the evening sun.

Cloverleaf Design

Materials and Tools Needed

Lumber: Composite stockade pickets
(3¹/₂ inches wide), composite dog-eared
pickets (7 inches wide). I used Fiberon
lumber for this project.
Tools: Table saw, drill press with hole saw
bit, hand drill.

In this example, I am using composite fence boards, which are made in earth tone colors. I am combining cool gray with a warm reddish brown. The design uses two commonly available picket tops, the pointed stockade and the dog-eared. You will only need to cut the pickets to the desired length and then cut a simple three-leaf clover window into the dog-eared pickets.

Cut all the pickets to the appropriate length.

The cloverleaf is formed by drilling three 2-inch diameter holes that slightly overlap each other. To do this, make a template from one of the dog-eared pickets. Make a mark 6 inches down from the top, centered on the picket. This mark will become the center top circle of the cloverleaf. Also make a mark at 7½ inches.

From the mark in the center of the picket, which is 7½ inches from the top, measure out ⅞ inch in either direction and make a mark. You now have three dots that span 1¾ inches.

Note: You could also use a copy of the cloverleaf pattern on page 201. The cloverleaf pattern has a red triangle imposed on top. The corners of the red triangle show the centers for each circle. You can mark to drill your pilot holes using the corners of the red triangle.

Use the pilot guide bit to carefully drill the center of all three marks, which you created in the prior two steps, to a depth of about ⅛ inch. Make sure you hit the center of your mark. You want the template accurate. It's fine if you are a tiny bit off when cutting individual picket windows, but this is the template from which all the pickets' cloverleaves will be cut.

When you are happy with your pilot holes, go a bit further and cut about ⅛ inch deep of the 2-inch diameter.

The circles on your template should overlay each other equally. If one circle appears to be farther apart than the other two, you should cut another template, especially if the problem is with one of the two lower circles. Slight differences in height on the two lower leaves will be more noticeable than a slight difference on the top centered leaf.

Take your dog-eared template and place it over top a regular dog-eared picket. Use a fine-tipped marker to make three dots through the center holes of your template. Your dog-eared picket should look like this when marked.

Use the dots as the centers for the three leaves of the cloverleaf window. Use the hole saw bit's pilot bit to pierce each dot. Continue to depress the drill press handle until you have cut a complete circle. Repeat for the remaining dots.

The cloverleaf window should be complete at this point. Do not worry too much if you were slightly off your mark on a few pickets. Minor differences here and there show that your pickets were individually created and give them character.

Now, attach the pickets to the rails. A little bit of space to permit expansion with changes in heat and humidity will reduce the stress on your fence components. Use shims, nails, screws, car keys, or any object as a spacer that will give you about an 1/8-inch gap between pickets.

For this design, there is a kickboard that runs between the posts. I used a 7-inch-wide fence board to make the kickboard. The kickboard overlaps the picket bottoms by 1 1/2 inches. Use screws to attach the kickboard onto the lower rail going through the picket.

Zigzag Design

Materials and Tools Needed

Lumber: 2 x 4 synthetic lumber for rails and separators, 2 x 2 synthetic lumber for pickets, 1 x 4 synthetic lumber for cleats (I used BJM Industries lumber).

Tools: Table saw (you can substitute a miter saw because there are no rip cuts required), hand drill, band saw (you can substitute a jigsaw because few cuts are needed).

This design has a very geometric flavor, with straight lines and numerous 45-degree angles. Its appearance has similarities to many inset-to-the-frame grid-style fences, but its construction is much simpler, with its infill attached to the sides of rails. The design is made by alternating shorter and taller square pale pickets. Each picket is separated from the next by a pair of parallelograms attached to the top and bottom rails. I made the pickets gray and the separators brown for color contrast.

For this design, each fence section measures 68 inches wide and uses twenty-eight separators. Use 2 x 4s that actually measure 1 1/2 x 3 1/2 inches to make the parallelogram separators. Cut the parallelograms with your table saw guide adjusted to a 45-degree angle. The long sides of the parallelogram will be 7 inches in length, so make marks on your 2 x 4 every 7 inches to produce parallelograms that look like this one when cut.

Cut the pickets to length and point the tops. Notice there are two different lengths to these pickets. The shorter pickets measure 39 inches and the taller pickets measure 43 inches. Cut each picket with a 45-degree point. Often square picket tops are cut on all four sides to form a pyramid top, but for this fence, cutting only two opposite sides looks best. I used seven long and six short pickets for each fence section. You will want to alternate between long pickets and short pickets to have the sections appear symmetrical between the posts.

Each fence section is 68 inches long, so cut the stringer to that length. For this fence I used decorative posts only at the corners and on the ends. For the run posts, I used a simple post with stringers mounted flush with the backs of the posts resting on simple rectangular cleats.

The cleats are placed with the tops parallel to the rails on the faux recessed panel posts.

Use exterior-grade screws to attach the top and bottom rails securely to the posts.

If the stringer is going to attach to a decorative faux recessed panel post, then cut a rabbet out of the end of the stringer. The rabbet will allow the stringer to rest on the panel separators while also wrapping around the stile of one of the corners of the decorative post. Cut the rail-end rabbet joint, removing 3/4 inch from the side and the end of the stringer.

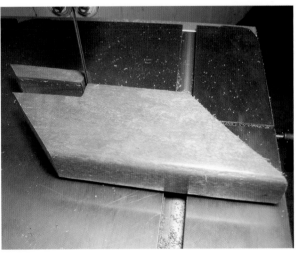

In each fence section, cut notches out of four of the parallelograms to allow them to rest on the cleats or faux rails on the posts. The notch should be the same depth as the cleat or faux rail.

Pick a post to work out from as you start attaching your infill. Use a screw to attach each separator, one on the top stringer and the other on the bottom stringer.

The separator should be attached so that a completely visible brown triangle will extend from the post to the first picket.

Attach the first tall picket next to the separator. The picket should extend 2 inches above the upper point of the parallelogram. Cut a small right triangle of lumber to have two sides 2 inches long. Use it as displayed to determine the correct height for each tall picket and attach the picket using a screw on each rail. Then attach a parallelogram on both the top and bottom rail to mirror the first parallelograms.

Attach a shorter picket on the downslope of the separator. The base of the point of this picket should be 2 inches higher than the lowest point of the parallelogram. Use your 2-inch right triangle as pictured to set the correct height of the picket. Attach the picket with a screw on both the top and bottom rails.

Use the techniques described in the prior steps to continue attaching the pickets and separators until you reach the next post.

Attach the final notched separators. You may need to trim these separators. The width of dimension lumber has slight differences from batch to batch. Those small variances may add up to 1/2 inch or even a whole inch by the time you reach the next post.

The completed fence has an interesting look from the rail side too. The parallelogram separators appear as triangles peaking up and poking down between each picket. If you prefer this look, you could achieve the same look on the front by placing a gray 1 x 4 board over the screw holes on the front of the fence and attaching it with exterior-grade finishing nails.

The completed fence looks even better if the screw holes are puttied over. The accenting terminal post with birdhouse finial detailed with a diamond-shaped door and little dormers on the roof is a fun accessory.

Filling Awkward Entrances: The Asymmetrical Sloping Gate

Materials and Tools Needed

Lumber: 2 x 4 lumber for frame, 2 x 10 lumber for frame, 2 x 2 lumber for lower brace, 1 x 4 lumber for infill (I used Eco-Tech synthetic lumber).
Tools: Band saw, table saw, hand drill.

Some gates are the centerpiece or crown jewel of the fence, other gates are meant to be inconspicuous or hidden. Then, there are those gates for awkward spaces. While they cannot be hidden, they do not need to draw undue attention to themselves either. They should be charming but subtle. Often an asymmetrical gate or a gate with gentle curves is the answer to these awkward cases.

The owner of this property is looking for a gate between the main house and one of the outbuildings for several reasons. The main house has an air-conditioning unit that he wants obscured from view. He wants visibility through the gate, but not enough to let the family dog slip through. The opening is only 33 inches wide at its narrowest point, so the owner thinks it would be nice if that entire width could be used by the gate without losing any of that opening space to posts. Finally, he wants the gate hinged to open against the main house, because there is a stepping-stone path leading away from it.

Notice the frame is made of three pieces. The bottom piece is a straight and simple 32-inch-long 2 x 4. The top piece starts off straight, but then slopes at about a 22½-degree angle. In addition to the angle, there is also a gentle curve to the slope. The diagonal middle piece also has a gentle slope. That diagonal piece makes this gate strong, efficiently transferring the gate's weight to the hinge side.

Start by making the top piece of the frame. Transfer a 22½-degree line to a 2 x 10 board. To make the line, fold a sheet of 8½x11 paper, as pictured, to make a 45-degree angle.

Fold it again by matching the two 45-degree sides together. Use this 22½-degree wedge to draw a 10-inch line on the end of your 2 x 10.

Make a parallel line 3½ inches below your first line. Make the line a bit longer than the upper line.

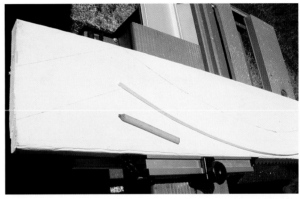

Use a draftsman's flexible curve to trace a curve starting at the elbow of where your upper parallel line and curve meet. Trace the line longer than you will need. Then measure 3½ inches below that curve at several places along the curve and make small pencil marks. Take your flexible curve and place it under the marks you just measured to make a parallel curve. When you are done you will have the outline of your upper frame rail.

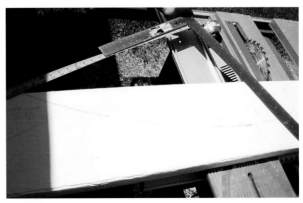

We know the gate needs to be 32 inches from one side to the other. The lower frame rail will be a straight cut 32 inches long. Extend the straight 10-inch line on top of the upper rail. From that extended line, drop a perpendicular line at 32 inches.

Hold your tape measure parallel to the upper straight line. Extend your tape measure to past 32 inches in length. Now keep it fixed in place.

Place a builder's square on your tape, keeping it centered on the tape as pictured. To give a little room for error, go an extra $1^1/2$ inches past the 32-inch mark to $33^1/2$ inches, and place the corner of the square at $33^1/2$ inches. The lower arm of the builder's square should be intersecting somewhere on the curved lines of the upper rail. Mark the cutoff line. (This rail will be about $1^1/2$ inches too long, but you will trim it later.)

Trace a line where the builder's square intersects with the upper rail's curves. Cut the extra wood from the end of your board on a table saw or with a circular saw so that you have less to deal with when you cut the upper rail on the band saw.

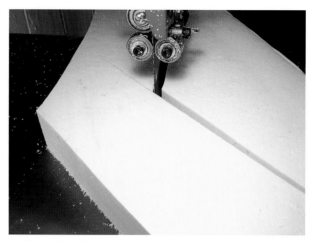

Use a band saw to cut out your upper rail. For the lower rail, cut a 2 x 4 to 32 inches long.

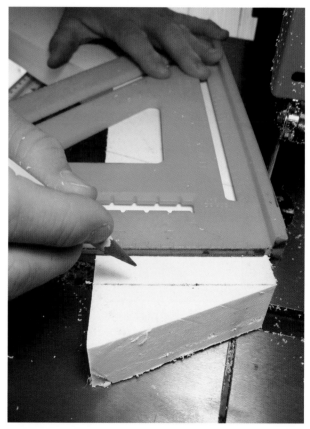

Mark and cut the straight end of the upper rail to make the end square.

This gate uses simple pickets. Use 1 x 4 boards and cut five 58-inch pickets. You can leave them straight, or you can add a simple scallop top to each picket. We will attach each picket with 2 inches of the picket above the top rail. Pickets that fall on the curved part of the rail will have one side 2 inches above and the other side will have even more above the rail.

Still on the hinge side of the gate, measure 28 inches down from the top of the top rail and make a mark on the picket. Align the top of the lower rail with the mark on the picket and attach the picket to the rail while keeping it square.

Lay your upper and lower frames on a flat surface and then use two pickets on either side of the frame. Lay your pickets with 2 inches extending above the rail. Place each picket 1/2 inch in from the edge of the rails. On the latch side, your upper rail is still not cut to size, so your picket will be more than 1/2 inch inset on the top curved rail. Attach the upper corner of the frame by screwing the hinge side picket to the top rail while keeping the two members square using a speed square.

Move to the bottom latch side of the frame. Keep the top of the picket 2 inches above the curved frame while squaring and attaching the bottom rail to the picket to connect the final square corner.

Because the upper rail attaches on the latch side along the curve, you cannot attempt to keep it square. Attach the upper curved rail to the picket with two screws and trim the excess off the curve. When completed the join should look like this.

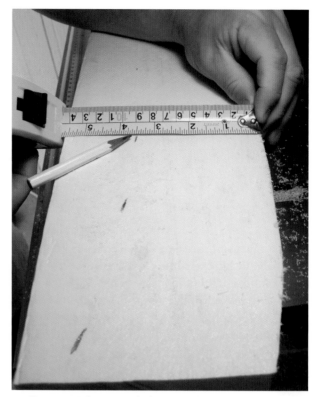

Cut a gently curved diagonal brace to transfer the weight from the latch side to the hinge side of the gate. If you can, use the scrap from above or below the curve you just cut for your upper rail. Make marks 3 1/2 inches away and parallel to your curved cut as pictured. Then use your flexible curve to connect those marks.

Evenly space your pickets and attach them, keeping the appropriate 2 inches above the top rail working from hinge side to latch side. When all the pickets are attached, trim the excess off the bottom of the pickets to make them all even.

Cut your brace on the band saw.

Flip your gate over so the rails are facing up.

Lay out your brace so that it looks pleasant and extends from the latch side to the hinge side. It does not have to go from edge to edge; you can set it in from the end. Use a short pencil and mark the undersides of the brace where they overlap the rails. Cut the braces at the marks.

Toe screw your brace to your frame. Use at least two screws on each end of the brace to attach the brace to the frame.

Attach a 2 x 2 brace across the lower portion of the gate to spread out vibration and reduce the ability for individual pickets to warp. Measure 10 inches from the bottom of the gate and attach the brace using screws.

Lay out the hinges on the gate. Drill holes for bolts. Buy sturdy hinges and heavy-duty square or hex-head screws like those pictured. Manufacturers often package the hinges with the bolts. The screws are usually a good length for the gate frame. But using these shorter screws on the post doesn't take advantage of the post's thickness and increases the chance that the screws on the post will pull out. For that reason I buy lag screws that will go deep into the post. The downside is that the lag screws need to be painted to match the hinges.

Prop the gate in the opening and drill the location for the lag screws. First drill a small hole, because it is easy to keep smaller holes accurate. Then drill a larger hole through the center of the small pilot hole.

Use a ratchet set or screwdriver to attach the lag screws. Don't use a drill at this point—you have greater control with a ratchet set, reducing the chances of stripping the hole or snapping the screw.

Here is the completed gate.

Creating Decorative Contrast:
The Combination Gate

Materials and Tools Needed

Lumber: 2 x 3 lumber for frame and
bracing, 2 x 10 lumber for pediment,
1 x 4 lumber for infill
(I used Eco-Tech synthetic lumber).
Tools: Band saw, table saw, hand drill.

Mark the stiles. The two stiles measure 36 inches and are cut from 2 x 3 lumber. They have decorative cut heads that face inward.

The stiles also have three 1$^{1}/_{2}$-inch-wide and $^{1}/_{2}$-inch-deep dados to receive the three rails. The bottom dado starts 33$^{1}/_{2}$ inches from the top and ends 1 inch from the bottom of the stile. The top dado starts 7 inches from the top of the stile and the middle dado starts 18 inches below the top of the stile.

L ike combination fences, combination gates use two or more styles of infill to form the design. This gate draws your eye with its gracefully scrolling top, picketed bottom, and zigzag grid middle. It combines inset infill with mounted infill to form a great focal point for a fence. The gate's frame is easy to customize. The basic structure can stay the same, but the profiles of the pediment, brackets, and pickets can be altered to make a gate that complements any fence or home style.

The gate does not feature the standard Z or X frames, but it is strong regardless. The gate's stiles are cut with $^{1}/_{2}$-inch dado joints to receive the three rails. The gate has a series of four boxes between the top and middle stiles. Those boxes are filled with a zigzagging set of braces that also provide structural support to the gate, transferring the weight to the hinged side. Between the middle and bottom stiles are a series of pickets. The middle stile has a rabbet the entire length of the stile. The tops of the pickets rest securely in this rabbet while their gently scalloped bottoms poke just below the lower rail.

Cut the decorative stile top on the band saw. Start with the shorter neck cut. Stop where it meets the head.

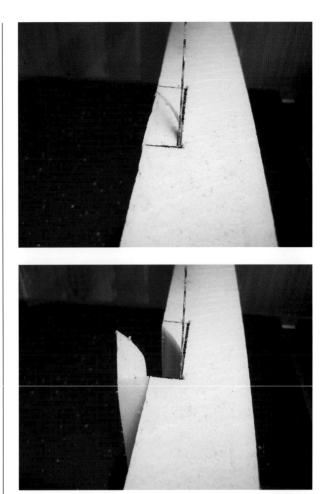

Start from the back of the head and continue cutting around the head until you reach the junction with the neck.

Cut until you can join your line and then follow the line to the corner of the dado until you cut away the lower part of the dado.

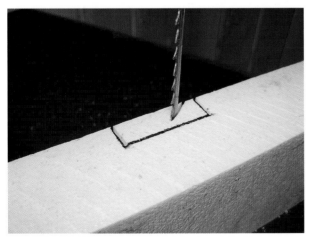

Cut the top dado joint's upper and lower 1/2-inch lines. Then start inside the upper portion of the dado and cut at an angle into it.

Turn the stile around and cut out the remaining piece of the dado.

When completed, the dado should look like this.

Cut the remaining dados in both stiles. When completed they should look like this.

Cut three 2 x 3 rails to 40 inches. For the middle rail, make a 3/4-inch rabbet the entire length of the rail to allow pickets to rest against. For the lower rail, make a parallel line 3/4 inches from the edge on the wide side of the rail.

You will need to strip off this 3/4 inch so your 1 x 4 pickets can overlap this rail without angling outward from the gate. While you could cut away this 3/4-inch strip for the entire length of your stile, if you use a band saw, you can cut in from the sides and leave 1/2 inch on each end uncut. This still makes room for your pickets but creates a nicer-looking, flush joint on the bottom stile and rail.

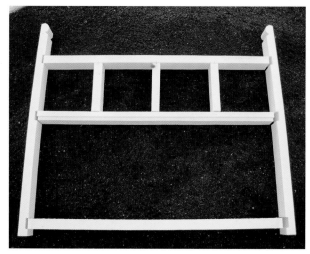

Cut three 81/2-inch-long 2 x 3s and evenly space them. Each box should be 81/2 inches wide in the void.

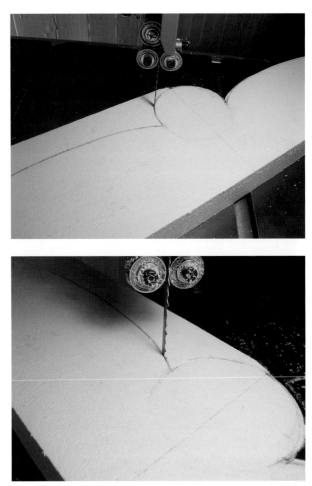

Screw the frame together while checking the frame for square.

Select, trace, and cut out your decorative scroll top pediment pattern. (See page 216 for patterns.)

When you have attached all the joints with screws, the frame should look like this.

Optional: If you have a drill press and rosette cutter bit, you may want to make a decorative rosette in your gate pediment. (See page 66 for making rosettes.)

Make a line down the middle of a 2 x 3 on the wide side. This 2 x 3 will be used to cut your four zigzag braces. (Use another 2 x 3 to balance the frame.)

Place one end of the 2 x 3 under the first box. Align the center mark on the 2 x 3 with the corners of the box. Now, outline with pencil where the edge of the box rests on your 2 x 3. Move your 2 x 3 to the next box and mark the second brace. Do this for all four boxes. Number the pieces as you go so that you can put them back in the box where you traced them.

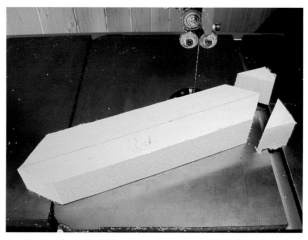

Cut out each of the four braces using a band saw.

Mark a decorative arch on one side of each of the braces.

Cut out the arch using a band saw.

Attach each brace with two screws.

Attach the braces with a decorative arch. Use 1x boards to lift the braces and make them about 3/4 inch inset to the frame.

Place the decorative pediment on the top of the gate. Use 1x boards on the ground to hold the pediment inset to the frame by 3/4 inch. Attach the pediment with screws from the top and the bottom to secure it.

Cut five pickets from 1 x 4 stock to 18 inches in length. Make a decorative scallop on the bottom of the pickets using an object that has a pattern that you like.

Use a band saw to cut the decorative bottoms of the pickets for the gate.

Mount the gate in the opening while keeping the gate level.

Attach one picket in the center of the gate and measure out an equal distance on either side of it. Place a picket on either side of your center picket at your measurement. Measure out the same distance again to place the two remaining pickets. The pickets for this gate were spaced at 3 1/2 inches.

Use blocks to raise the gate to the height of the hinges.

Use shims to keep a space between the gate and the hinge post while you attach the hardware. (This is a replacement for an existing gate, so the hinges are already in place on the post and the frame was constructed to fit the current hinge placement.)

Here is the completed gate. Its decorative braces and broad pickets contrast beautifully against the slender pales of the picket fence.

Making a Complementary Gate

Materials and Tools Needed

Lumber: 2 x 4 lumber for frame and
bracing, 2 x 2 lumber for infill.
Tools: Table saw, hand drill.

Y ou may want to make a gate that complements
a fence. Here's an extraordinarily simple and
lightweight design that's easy to build. The gate
gets its strength from three rails, three long pickets,
and a two-piece diagonal brace that is separated by
the middle rail. The rest of the gate infill is medium
and short sawtooth pickets.

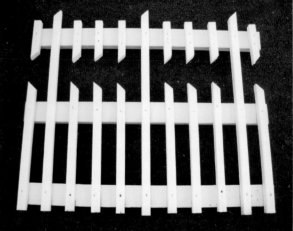

Cut three 42-inch rails. Center and attach one of the
three long pickets on the rails. Measure and mark $2^3/4$
inches in each direction from the center picket on each
rail. Place and attach the short picket at the mark on the
top rail and medium-length pickets on the middle and
bottom rails. Keep measuring out $2^3/4$ inches and lay
the pickets until the infill looks as pictured.

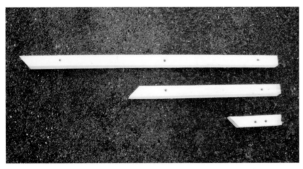

Cut three long 2 x 2 pickets to $34^1/2$ inches. Drill pilot holes in the long pickets starting from the bottom at
3 inches, 16 inches, and $29^1/4$ inches. Then cut eight
medium-length 2 x 2 pickets to $20^1/2$ inches. Drill pilot
holes in them at 3 inches and 16 inches from the bottom.
Finally, cut eight short pickets of $7^1/2$ inches. Drill pilot
holes in them at $2^1/4$ inches and $3^3/4$ inches from the
bottom. *Note*: For an even firmer gate, replace the out-
ermost sets of short- and medium-length pickets with
a long picket on each end.

Turn the gate over.

Check the gate for square. Then lay a 2 x 4 diagonally from the top latch side of the gate to the bottom hinge side of the gate.

Use a short pencil and mark the underside of the 2 x 4 to cut two diagonal braces between the three rails. Cut the braces at your marks using a table saw or circular saw.

Use 3¹/₂-inch-long screws to attach the braces to the rails.

When the braces are attached, the gate should look as pictured and be fixed square.

The completed gate beautifully complements the fence infill with a light look and a sturdy frame.

Use blocks and shims to adjust the gate to its appropriate height between the gate posts. Attach the gate hinges and latch hardware.

Encasing Posts

Materials and Tools Needed

Lumber: 4 x 4 lumber for core post and finial, 1 x 4 lumber for encasement, 1 x 6 lumber for encasement, 5/4 x 6 lumber for post cap (I used BJM industries synthetic lumber).
Tools: Table saw, drill press, hand drill, band saw.

Ornamental posts are a great way to accent your fence. Encased posts make a structurally small post look larger. This post appears to be 5 inches square, but it actually has a smaller core post that measures $3^1/2$ x $3^1/2$ inches. It has been encased with 1x lumber to make the aboveground portion appear larger.

The impact of this ornamental post is bold. The round rosette and the long bevel-shaped appliqué cast their shadows on the post body, making them stand out. The top of the post is capped, molded, and then crowned with an impressive-looking finial.

For this design, the core post measures 7 feet long. Of that length, 3 feet will be anchored in the ground. The 4-foot aboveground portion will be encased in 1x lumber. Most 1x lumber is $3/4$ inches thick. Most 4 x 4 posts are $3^1/2$ inches square. So our $3^1/2$-inch post, encased on all four sides with $3/4$ inch lumber, will become a 5-inch-square post.

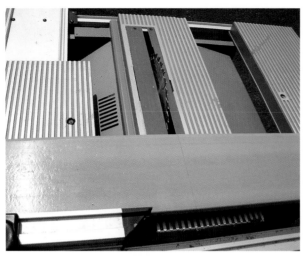

Cut two 1 x 4 boards to 4 feet and two 1 x 6 boards to 4 feet.

Put one of the 1 x 6 boards on a flat surface, lay the post on the 1 x 6, and place the two 1 x 4s on either side of the post. Notice that the 1 x 6 is about 1/2 inch too wide to be flush with the edges of the 1 x 4s. You will need to trim 1/2 inch off the 1 x 6s. If your 1 x 6 has rounded edges like this one does, trim 1/4 inch from each side of the 1 x 6 to keep all four corners consistently sharp. If you rip 1/2 inch from only one side of the 1 x 6s you will have two sharp corners and two rounded corners on your post.

Again, put one of the 1 x 6s on a flat surface, lay the post on the 1 x 6, and place the two 1 x 4s on either side of the post. This time the trimmed 1 x 6s should be flush with the edges of the 1 x 4s. Use eight screws, two per board, all around the top of the post to attach each board to the core post.

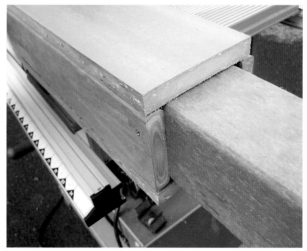

Then go the bottom of the encased part of the post. Again, use eight screws, two per board, all around the base of the encased portion of the post to attach the boards to the core post.

Lumber thicknesses can vary. Ideally, a 4 x 4 post encased in 1x lumber on all four sides should measure exactly 5 inches square. If your lumber is thicker or thinner, you will need to adjust the measurements in later steps to accommodate the thickness of the lumber you are using.

To add more visual weight to the top of the post, you will add another layer of encasement below the post cap. Cut 1 x 6 boards to encase the upper portion of the post in a manner similar to how you just encased the overall post. For this post, I cut a 1 x 6 board into two 5-inch-long pieces and two 6 1/2-inch-long pieces and attached them using screws, flush with the post top.

A question you need to ask yourself is how much of the post detail work do you want to do before the post is set in the ground? The more pieces you apply, the more that tends to be in the way while you are leveling and setting your post. I prefer to add post caps, finials, appliqués, and other fine work that will be held on with only finishing nails after I set the post. In this example the post cap molding is a large and simple box held on securely with screws. If I had used a finer post cap molding held on with finishing nails, I would have waited to apply it until after the post was set.

Optional Modifications

Encased posts frequently have kickboards, rails, or stiles inset to the post. I am going to show you how to do some minor modifications to this post to allow it to receive the kickboard and pre-assembled rail and stile frame of the quatrefoil lattice fence. We are going to make a decorative terminal post customized for the fence.

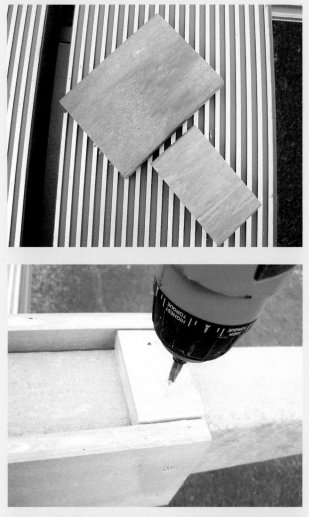

Remove one of the 1 x 4s encasing the post. Cut two smaller pieces of 1 x 4, one measuring 4³/4 inches long and the other 2 inches long.

Attach the 2-inch piece flush with the encased portion of the bottom. This small piece at the bottom will function as a cleat holding the weight of the kickboards and the fence infill. Attach the 4³/4-inch piece flush with the top using two screws.

The stiles and rail of the quatrefoil lattice are 3¹/2 inches wide, so they will take up the entire width of the core post. The kickboard is only 1¹/2 inches wide. The finished fence's kickboard will be 7 inches high and flush with the front of the fence infill, so we need to cut a filler block made of 1x stock that will measure 7 inches high and 2 inches wide. Attach the filler block with two screws.

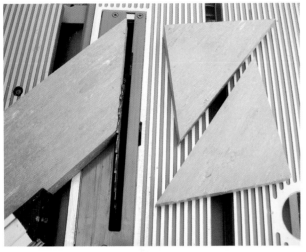

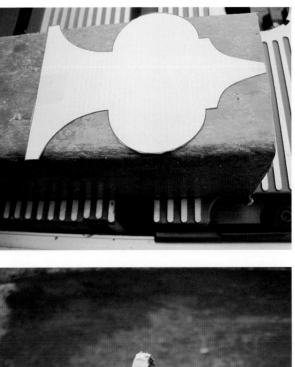

A simple square-cut board is often enough to make an attractive post cap. For this post, a 7-inch-square post cap will be attractive while providing an appropriately sized platform to display the post finial. With the exception of the post cap, I did not need any stock that was 7 inches or wider to make the post. So, I didn't order a 1 x 8 to make my post cap. Not to worry: if you want to make a larger post cap using smaller lumber, you can cut two triangles of lumber from a board at a 45-degree angle by adjusting your table saw. Here I have cut two right triangles from a 5-inch-wide board. The triangles measure about $7^1/_{16}$ inches on their two shorter sides and exactly 10 inches on their long side. Glue the triangles together on their longer sides to form a $7^1/_{16}$-inch square post cap.

Review the finial cutting project instructions and the finial patterns on page 210. Select a pattern to your liking; for this finial I used the pattern on page 212. Cut the finial.

Using 1 x 4 material, cut this rosette design using the rosette cutter on the drill press.

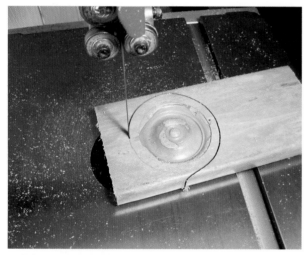

Then trace a larger circle around the rosette and cut it out of the stock using the band saw. Decide which sides of the post you plan to decorate and cut enough rosettes to do each side.

Adjust your table saw blade to cut a 45-degree bevel.

Use your saw's rip fence and rip two bevels that are 1 1/2 inches on each side from a 2 x 4. (You will end up with three bevels including the middle piece).

The two smaller bevels have two sides that measure 1 1/2 inches and will be used for this project. The remaining large bevel can be saved to use on another project.

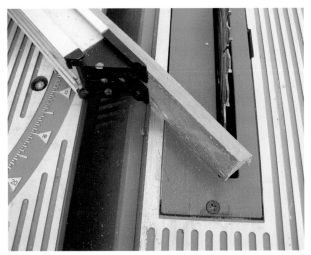

Cut a 45-degree angle on the end of the bevel strip you just made. To do this, adjust your table saw blade to its upright position.

Now adjust your sliding guide to a 45-degree angle so that you can hold the lumber against the guide as you cut the tip of the bevel off to make a prism end on your appliqué.

Measure and mark 24 inches from the cut end. Flip the lumber around and make another pass on your mark. You should have a completed prism appliqué like the two pictured here.

Cut as many prism appliqués as you will need to adorn each face of the post that have an appliqué. At this point, you should have all the pieces you need to detail your encased post. It is time to set the posts and make the fence. Once the fence is set, you can add the finishing details to your posts.

Measure 4 inches down from the post cap molding and attach your rosette with a finishing nail on the center of the post.

Measure 3 inches below your rosette and install your prism panel appliqué using finishing nails. Repeat for each side that you plan to decorate with your appliqués.

Mark the center on the top of the post cap and the bottom of your finial.

Drill a hole in the post cap and finial to allow a dowel screw to connect your post cap to your finial. Attach the post cap to your post with four screws or nails. Keep them in the area that will be hidden under your finial. Insert the dowel screw into your finial and screw your finial onto your post cap. Use finishing nails on one of the sides of your finial to make it difficult to unscrew the finial from the post cap.

Here is the completed encased post with detail pieces.

Dressing Up the Fence: The Faux Recessed Panel Post

Materials and Tools Needed

Lumber: 4 x 4 lumber for core post and finial, 4 x 4 lumber for corner stiles, 1 x 4 lumber for post rails, 1 x 6 lumber for post rails, 5/4 x 6 lumber for post cap (I used BJM Industries synthetic lumber).
Tools: Table saw, hand drill, band saw.

Ornamental posts are a great way to accent your fence. The faux recessed panel post is a classic design that adapts to many types of fences. This post appears to be a $5^1/4$-inch-square post, but it actually has a smaller core post that measures $3^1/2$ x $3^1/2$ inches. It has been encased with 1x lumber and modified 2x lumber to make the aboveground portion appear larger.

The finished post is attractive with its slender upright lines. At its core is a 4 x 4 brown post, but it has been partially encased in gray lumber. The gray lumber has been applied to the post in the form of long, vertical corner stiles and short, wide horizontal rails. In addition to being attractive, the horizontal rails can also be used to support the infill of your fence. The top of the post is capped and molded with a charming birdhouse finial. This post may look complex, but you will see it is not as convoluted as it first appears.

We need to strip away the finial can cap and examine just the core post and its encasement. For this design the core post is $3^1/2$ inches square and 7 feet long. Of that length, 3 feet will be anchored in the ground. The 4-foot aboveground portion will be encased in modified 2 x 2 lumber and 1x lumber. The 2x lumber has been modified to remove a $5/8$-inch rabbet from one edge, leaving $7/8$ inch to rise off the post. That rabbet is then placed over the corner of the core post. Most 1x lumber is $3/4$ inch thick. That makes it about $1/8$ inch narrower than the lumber sticking out from the corner. There is a reason for this.

Stiles and rails can be completely flush with each other and that creates an acceptable appearance. Also acceptable is to have rails thinner than stiles. However, rails thicker than stiles look odd and should be avoided. The problem with making rails and stiles flush is that it requires a great deal of precision in your lumber widths and cuts. For that reason, it is more forgiving to have the rails slightly thinner than the stiles. That is what I have done here.

Finally, the stiles and rails are encased in a 1 x 2 post cap molding.

Place your stiles flush with the top of the post.

Set up your table saw blade and rip fence to allow you to take off a 5/8-inch rabbet. To make more accurate rabbets, work with a helper who will pull the stock through when it is over halfway. Then take a push stick and keep the stock against the rail and down on the table as the helper pulls the stock. When the stock has only 6 inches left to cut, travel with it. This keeps the lumber tight to the fence and table without slipping off and cutting the push stick, or worse.

Mount them by inserting a screw 1 inch from the top of the post, sunk diagonally from the corner of the stile into the core post. Also screw 1 inch from the base of the aboveground portion of the post. Do this for all four stiles.

Cut the stiles from your modified 2 x 2s to 4 feet in length. You will need four stiles for this post.

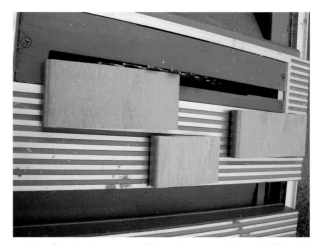

For this design you will need a top rail, a middle rail, and a bottom rail. Cut all rails to the distance between the stiles. For this post that distance is 2 1/4 inches. For the upper and lower rails cut from a 1 x 6 board. For the middle rail, cut from a 1 x 4 board.

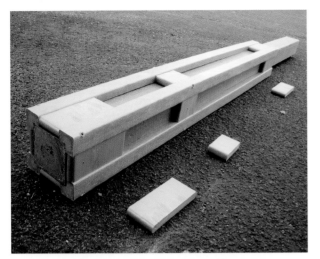

Attach with screws or finishing nails.

Cut a post cap molding from 1 x 2 stock.

Cut two pieces to $5^{1}/_{4}$ inches to be flush with the edge of the post and cut two more pieces to $6^{3}/_{4}$ inches. For the shorter pieces, I find it easier to attach them if I shave away a bit of the board's inside corner so that it does not come in contact with the screws holding the stiles.

Use finishing nails to attach the post cap molding flush with the top of the post as shown.

Cut a 7^1/$_{16}$-inch-square post cap to apply over the top of the post. Use four screws to attach this post cap. Locate the screws to be hidden by your finial.

To make a simple gabled finial, adjust your table saw to a 45-degree angle and cut a pointed top on a piece of 4 x 4 lumber.

Measure 5^1/$_4$ inches from the top of the gable and mark a line to cut off the finial from the 4 x 4. Pictured are two cut gable finials.

To make the roof, use a 1 x 4 board and rip a 45-degree angle from the edge. Crosscut the board into 4^1/$_2$-inch-long boards. Center the boards on either side of the finial top. Attach with finishing nails.

Here is the completed gable finial with accenting roof and post cap.

Optional Modifications

Gable finials are not very hard to make and they look great. They can also be customized further to mimic elements of your house or garden. The following example dresses up a simple gabled finial by making it look like a birdhouse with dormers.

To make the dormers, take some of the leftover 2 x 2 stiles from making the post. Use the band saw to cut the ends off at a 45-degree angle.

Then cut two small 1/4-inch-thick squares from a 2 x 2.

Attach the dormers to opposite sides of the gabled roof finial and add square doors diagonally below the gables. The completed post with detail pieces is shown with a coordinating fence design.

Alternate version: Faux Raised Panel Post

In this variation of a built-up post, 2 x 2s are again used as the corner stiles, 2 x 4s are used as the rails, and 1 x 4s with molded edges are placed between the stiles and rails to create raised panels.

The components are all screwed or nailed to the surface of the post.

When assembling this post, attach rails and panels to the core post surface first, using a single screw for each rail or panel. Then place the stiles on the corners.

Panels and rails will provide support for the corner stiles. Screw the 2 x 2 stiles to the core post. Screw from the outer corner of the stile to the inner corner of the stile to penetrate the outer corner of the edge of the core post. You can also screw the stile to the rails.

In this design, it is not necessary to rabbet the stiles as they were for the faux raised panel version. Putting and painting your screw holes after completion will hide the fastener heads and improve the appearance.

Designs

A fence does not exist in a void. Sidewalks, pathways, trees, flowers, yards, houses, and streetscapes are part of picture when you view a fence. A photo of a mediocre fence among lush summer foliage and mature trees in a neighborhood with huge front lawns may look better than a photo of an exquisite fence in a less attractive setting. The drawings in this chapter provide an apples-to-apples comparison between fences. With landscaping and buildings stripped away, you can judge each design for appearance and function on its own merits.

Simple Picket Fences

Alternating Sawtooth

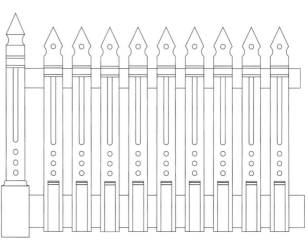

Birdhouse Tips

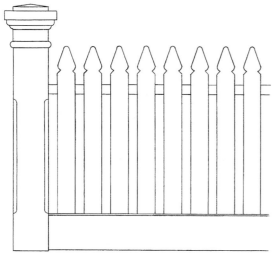

Blunted Arrow

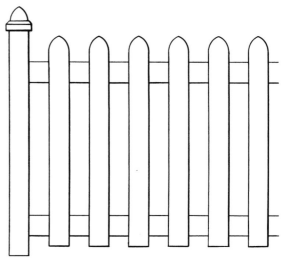

Cardinal Gothic Picket Fence

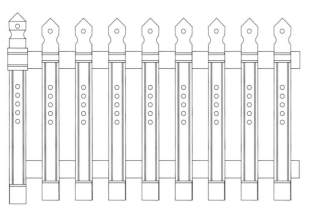

Buttoned Birdhouse

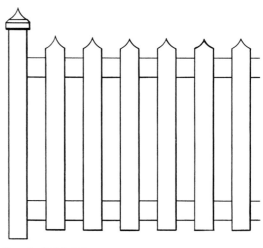

Serrated Picket Fence

Diamond-Head Picket Fence

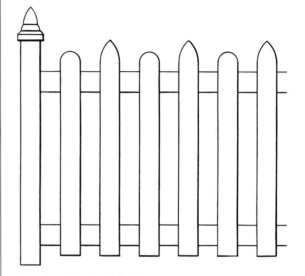

Round and Gothic Picket Fence

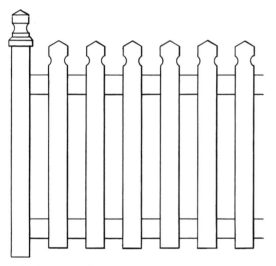

Whistle-Stop Picket Fence

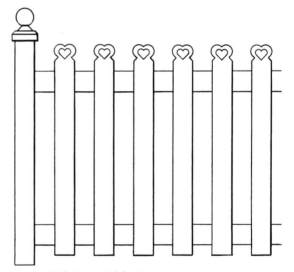

Sweet Little Hearts Picket Fence

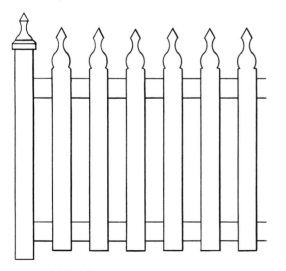

Sawn-Finial Picket Fence

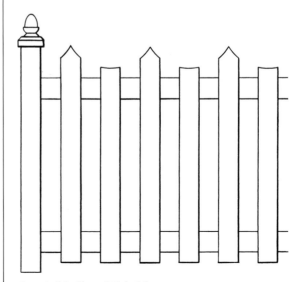

Serrated Scalloped Picket Fence

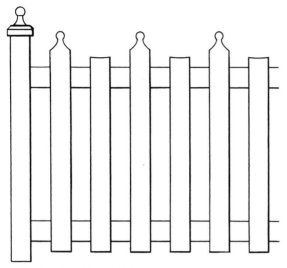

Orb-Tipped Scalloped Picket Fence

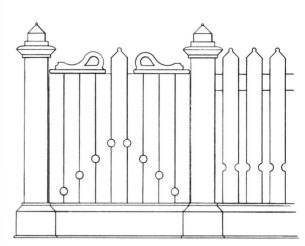

Nipple-Topped Narrow Picket Fence

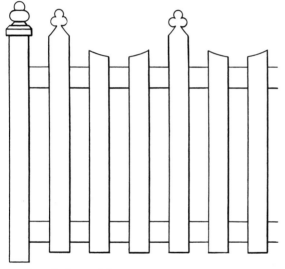

Scalloped Clover Picket Fence

V-Grooved Picket Fence

Handle-Topped Picket Fence

Winged Diamond Fence

Nipple-Topped Broad Picket Fence

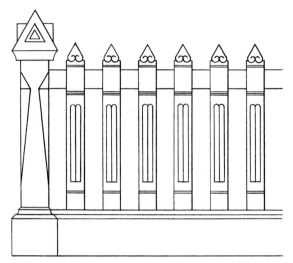

Sweetheart Chapel Picket Fence

Cherry Picket Fence

Ladyfinger Picket Fence

Scalloped Fence with Imitation Post

Simple Adam's Apple Fence

Ornate Classical Fence

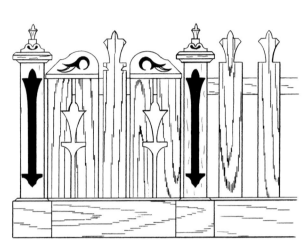

Trumpet-Topped Picket Fence

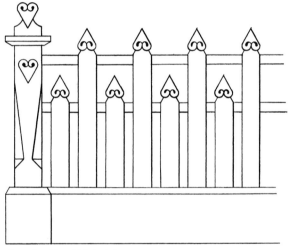

Shooting Heart Picket Fence

Board Fences

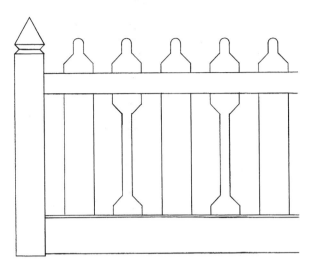

Alternating Lean and Broad

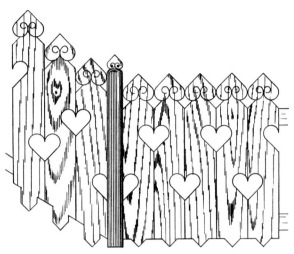

Pigtail Hearts Fence

Pointed Pisces

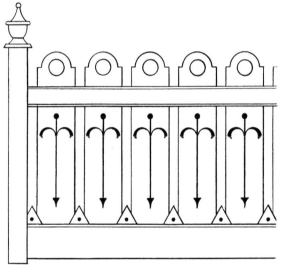

Winged Arrow Board Fence

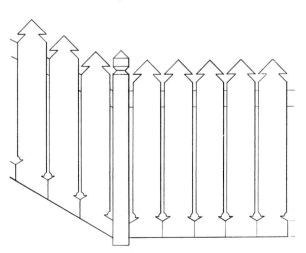

Flat Arrow Fence

Folk Board Fence

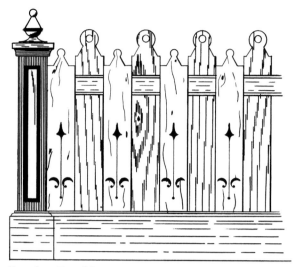

Board-on-Board Fence

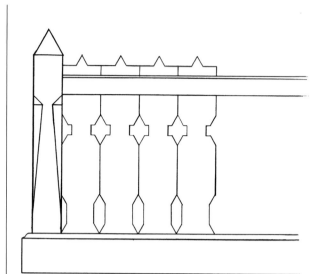

Neo-Egyptian Board Fence

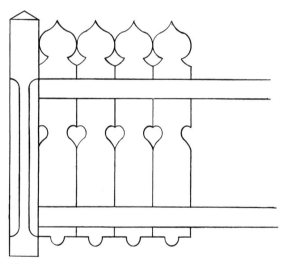

Pleasantly Plump Country Hearts Fence

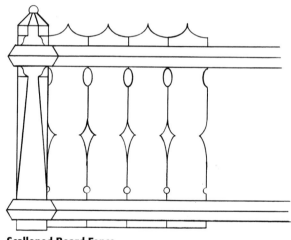

Scalloped Board Fence

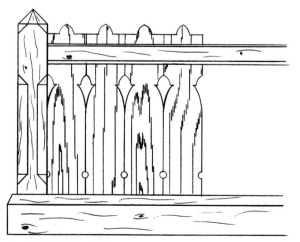

Rural Gothic Board Fence

Bleeding Hearts Fence

Lady Clovers

Popsicle Sticks

Weeping Arrows

Heavy Bulbs

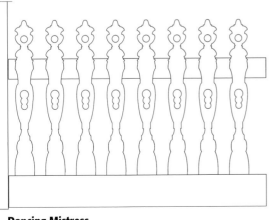

Dancing Mistress

Portal Windows

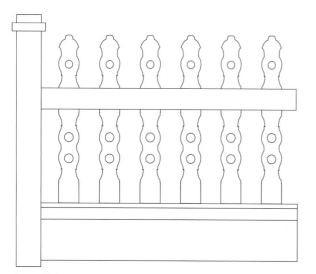

Loop-D-Loo

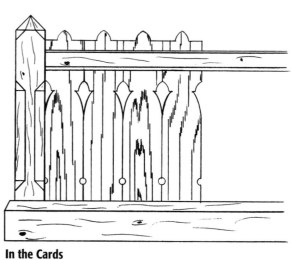

In the Cards

McHenry Delight

Autumn Leaves

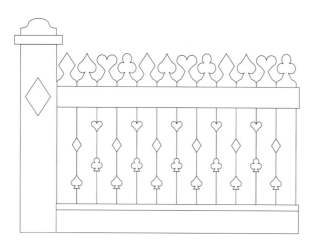

Decked-Out Pickets

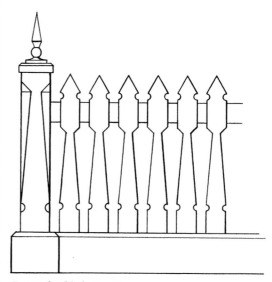

Tapered Whistle-Top Fence

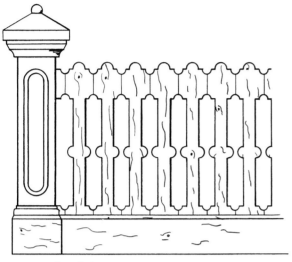

Over-Under Circle Fence

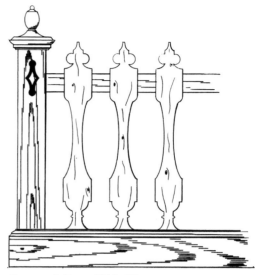

Gooseneck Spaced Picket Fence

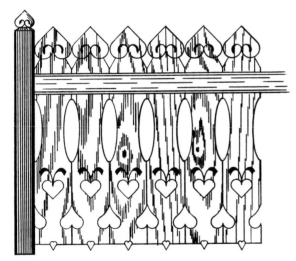

Folk Heart Fence

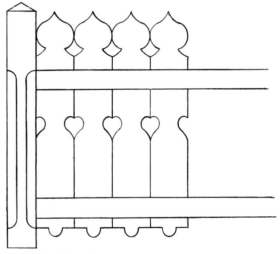

Clover-Top Picket Fence

Smiling Hearts Fence

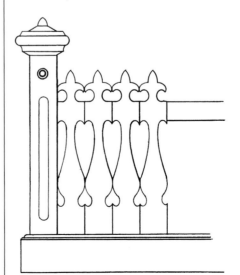

Fleur-de-lis Picket Fence

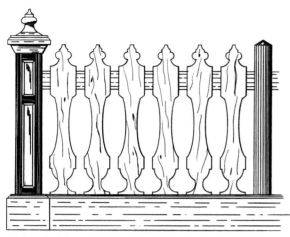

Pedestal Picket Fence

Ball-Topped Chamfered Picket Fence

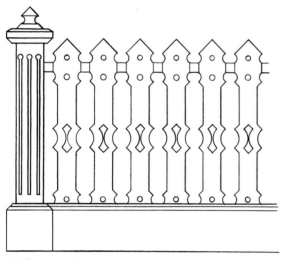

Birdhouse Picket Fence

Wren House Picket Fence

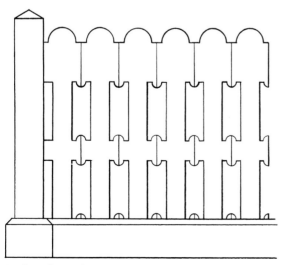

Scalloped Board Fence

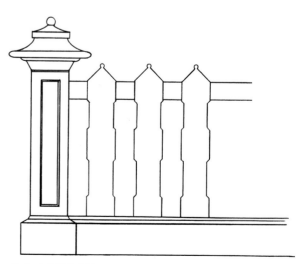

Oriental Picket Fence

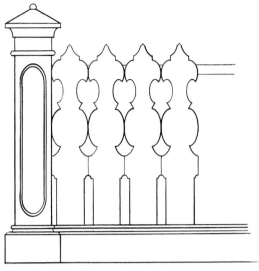

Gingerbread Gothic Fence

Storybook Gingerbread Fence

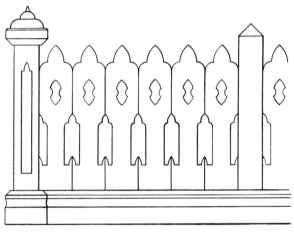

Chapel Gothic Fence

Alpine Gothic Fence

Peek-a-Boo Picket Fence

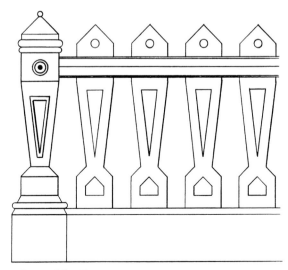

Salmon Picket Fence

Potbelly Picket Fence

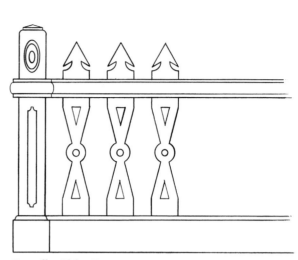

Propeller Picket Fence

Trumpet-Topped Picket Fence

Spade-Topped Picket Fence

Medallioned Balustrade Picket Fence

Balustrade Fences

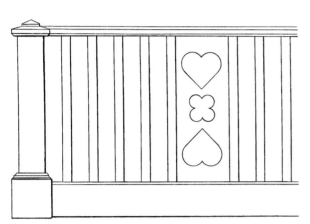

Board and Baluster

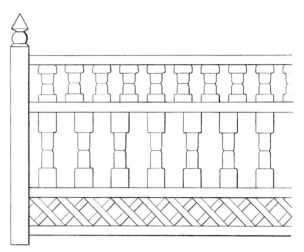

Layered Balustrade

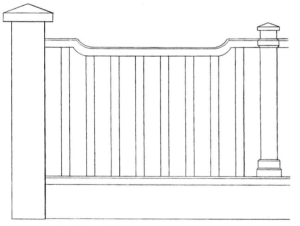

Gooseneck Balustrade

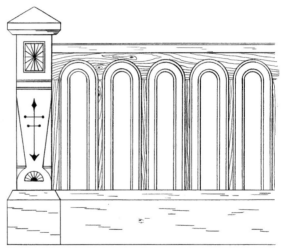

Roman Arches

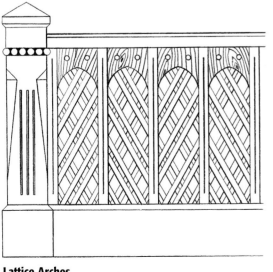

Lattice Arches

Serpentine Hearts

Scrolling Footed Hearts

Stout Balustrade

Drips and Drops

Neoclassical Fence

Bulbous Balusters

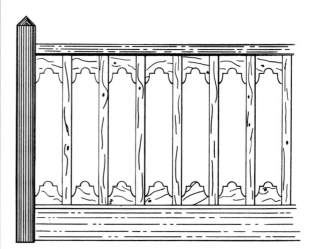

Running Gingerbread Fence

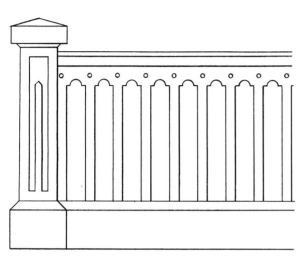

Columned Balustrade Fence

Gothic Fret Design Fence

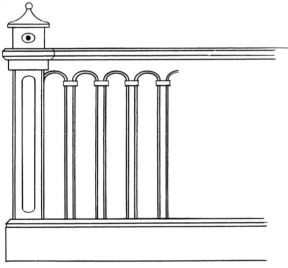

Oriental Balustrade Fence

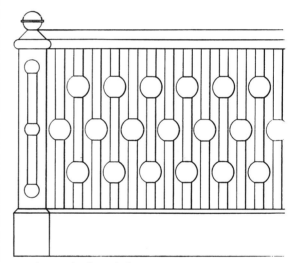

Mock Oversized Beaded Fence

Neo-Ionian Balustrade Fence

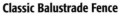

Classic Balustrade Fence

Veranda Balustrade Fence

Grid-and-Panel Fences

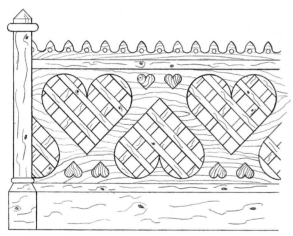

Loving Lattice

Five-Circle Whirl-Wheel Grid Fence

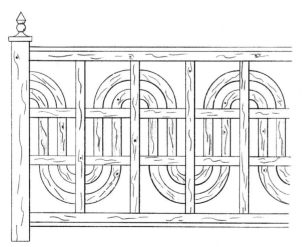

Flowing Font

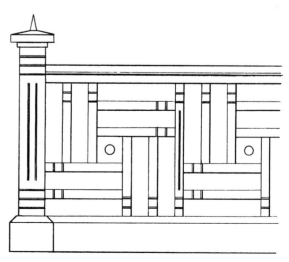

Double Whirl-Wheel Bull's-Eye Fence

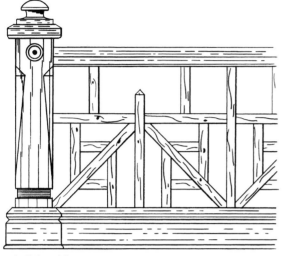

Obelisk Grid Fence

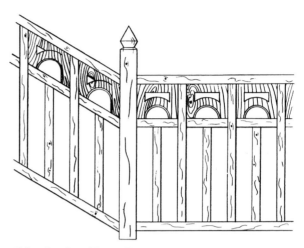

Rising-Sun Panel Insert Fence

Cross-Your-Heart Fence

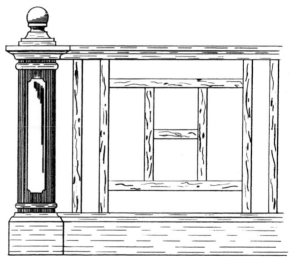

H Grid Fence

Shoelaced Hidden Hearts Fence

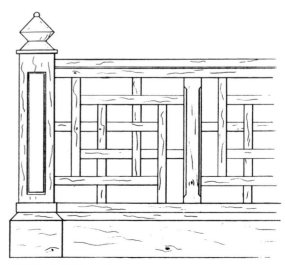

Grid Basket-Weave Fence

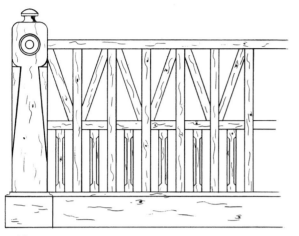

Grid V-Span Fence

Eastlake Elongated Tee

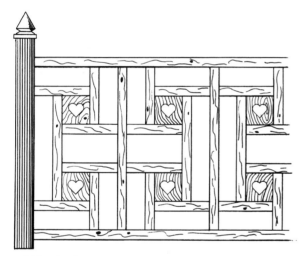

Whirl-Wheel Hearts Fence

Bric-a-Brac Collage Fence

Triple Whirl-Wheel Grid Fence

Kaleidoscope Fence

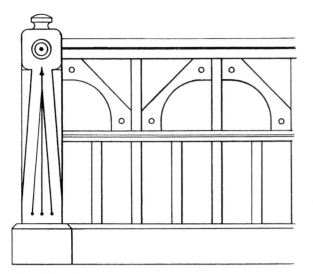

Cross-Brace Fence

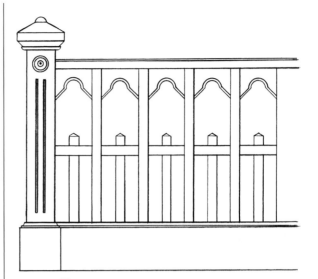

Neo-Gothic Fence

Country Morning Gothic Fence

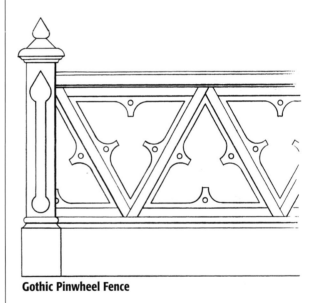

Gothic Pinwheel Fence

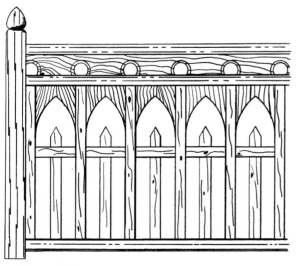

Gothic Revival Fence

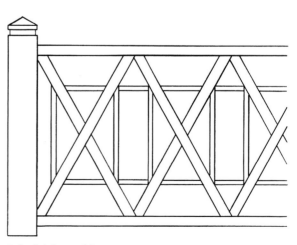

Colonial Crossed Fence

Halo Fence

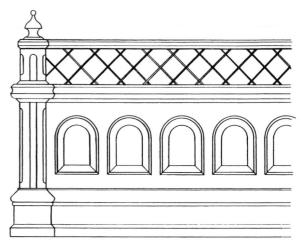

Cathedral Panel Fence

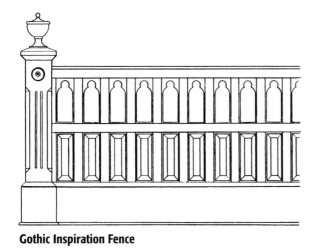

Gothic Inspiration Fence

Pale Fences

Rounded Pales with Faux Post

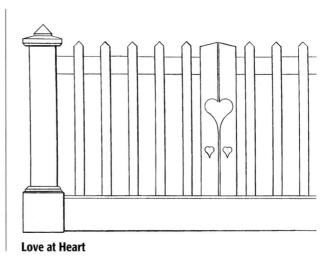

Love at Heart

Reverse Sawtooth

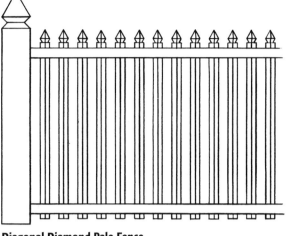

Diagonal Diamond Pale Fence

Classic Alternating-Picket Fence

Classic Alternating-Pale Fence

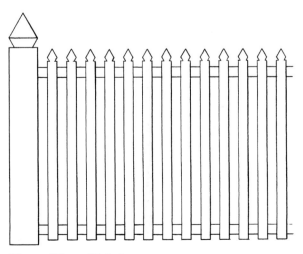

Diamond-Topped Pale Fence

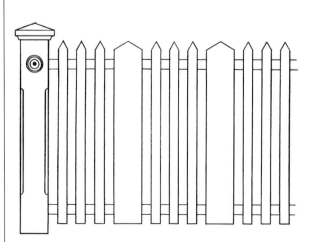

Alternating Picket and Board Fence

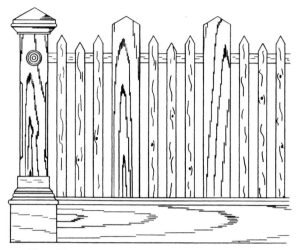

Peaking Picket Fence

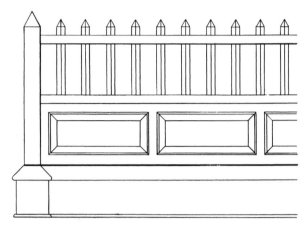

Pales and Lattice Fence

Windowed Board Fence

Pales and Card Suit Fence

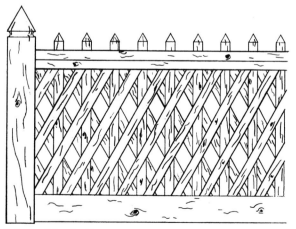

Pales and Lattice Fence

Patterns

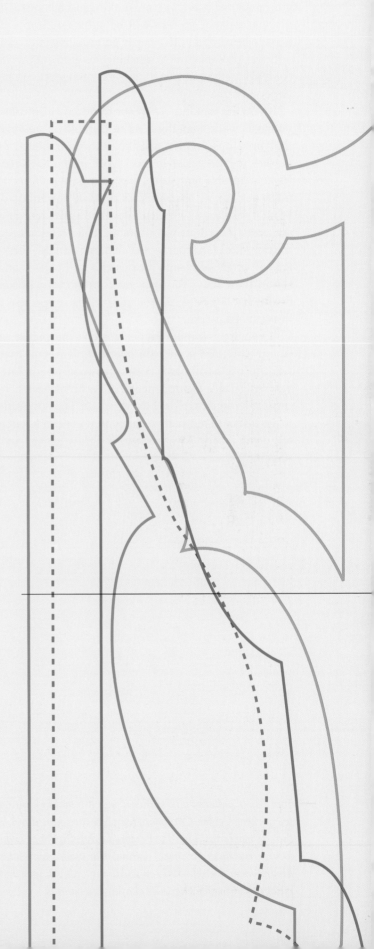

Some people have the gift of being able to look at a picture and draw a near-accurate rendition of what they see. But not all of us are that fortunate. For that reason this chapter provides several full-sized patterns.

One of the easiest ways to make a beautiful fence is to choose one interesting picket pattern. Pickets with space between them are the easiest to lay out and attach while getting attractive results. It does not matter whether the entire picket body has cutouts or just the top.

You can trace or copy the patterns in this book for your personal use. If you are making just a handful of pickets, a paper pattern will be sufficient. You will need to be careful with a paper pattern, however, as it will not provide much resistance as you follow its contours with your pencil. It is easy to crease or tear paper patterns.

If you are making dozens or hundreds of pickets, you will want something more durable. A material that provides greater resistance to your pencil or marker will be easier to work with in the long run. Make a durable template using your pattern. I like to make most of my templates out of white poster board. I find it easy to cut with a scissors and craft knife, and the poster board provides much greater resistance to the pressure of the marker than a paper pattern. Markers will often bleed onto the poster board pattern and soften the edges. You may need to let your poster board dry out between tracing pickets if you use a heavy bleed marker.

If you are going to rout designs on your picket, or if you just want a very durable template, you may want to use hardboard. With a hardboard template, you will be able to apply pencil pressure without concern for tearing or folding the template. The downside to a hardboard template is that you will need to cut it out using a band saw, fretsaw, or jigsaw instead of a scissors.

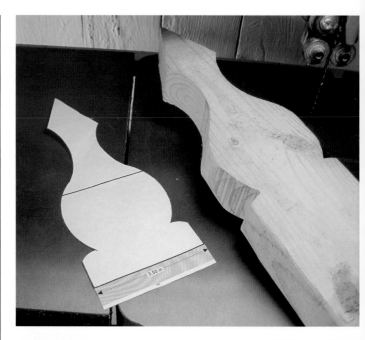

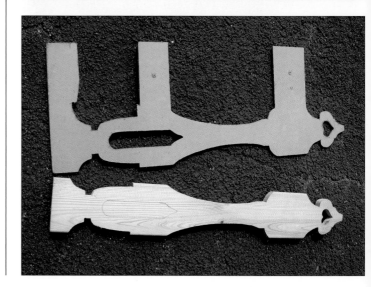

Top: Paper patterns will suffice if you are making only a few pickets. Center: Cardboard templates are more durable than paper, but still need to be stored carefully if you want to preserve them for reuse. Bottom: Hardboard templates are the most durable. You can use them with a router and pattern bit to make engraved shapes and cutouts.

Modifying Patterns

When you select your pattern, examine it for features that will be difficult to cut. Can you simplify the pattern to make the cut easier? Often you can make minor modifications to the pattern for ease in cutting that will not significantly change the appearance of the finished piece.

Patterns are most efficiently used with a band saw. Sometimes the throat of the band saw will get in the way of your cut. I found that I can change the pattern to make the cut easier with no negative impact to the appearance of the final picket.

You will want to make the majority of your cuts without needing to make relief cuts. These are cuts made into the scrap portion of the lumber, allowing those pieces to fall away as you cut your pattern. This gives you more room to cut your piece of lumber without binding the blade because of the tight radius of the curve you are cutting. If you need to make many relief cuts, you may want to consider using a smaller blade that can make tighter curves.

Some turns and angles may be so tight that even with a narrow blade, it is very difficult to cut out the shape without making several cuts. Here is where making minor changes to the cutout shape can be used to ease your job.

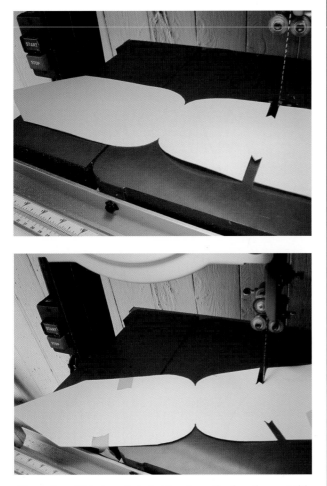

Above top: This template laid out on the band saw table shows that the side to the picket top is against the throat of the band saw before the blade even enters the cutout area. Above: In this second version of the same pattern, the slanted cutout can be made with ease. The point does not hit the throat of the band saw.

The two patterns are not significantly different in appearance, but the pattern with slanted cutouts is significantly easier to cut on the band saw.

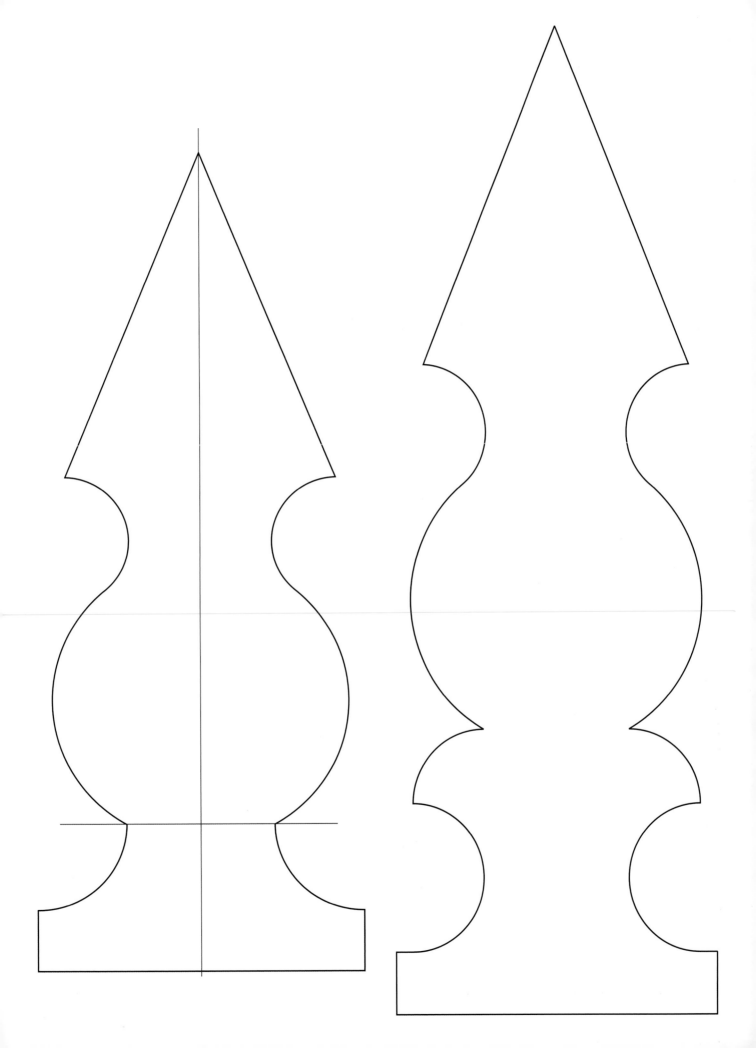

4.00 in

3.50 in

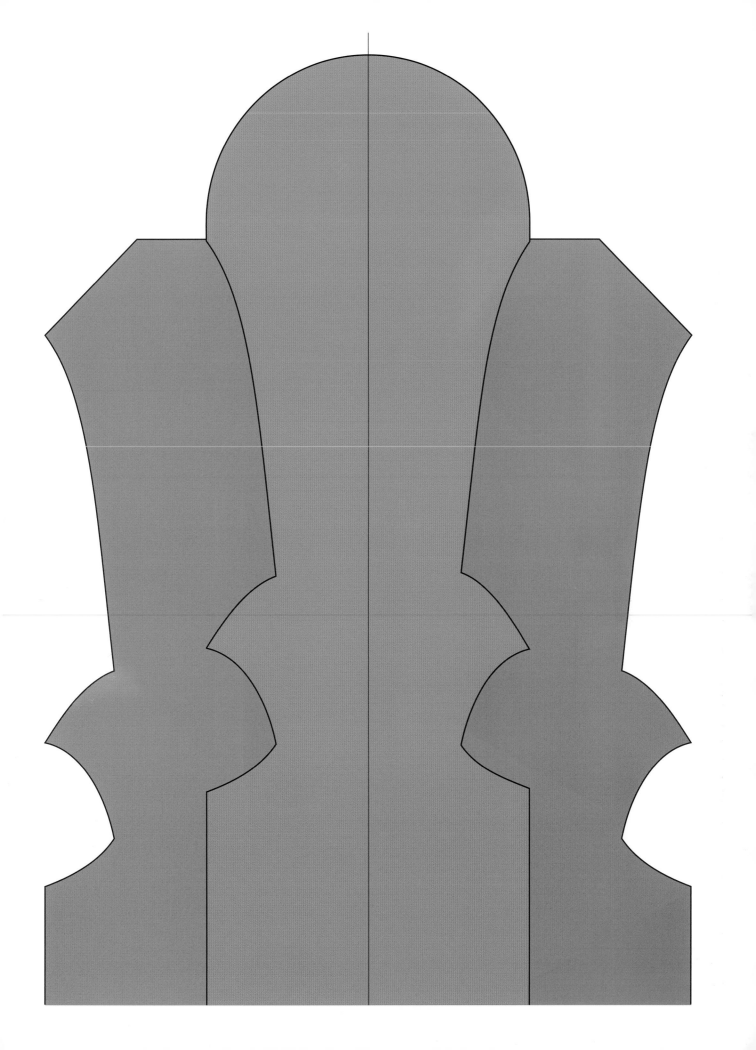

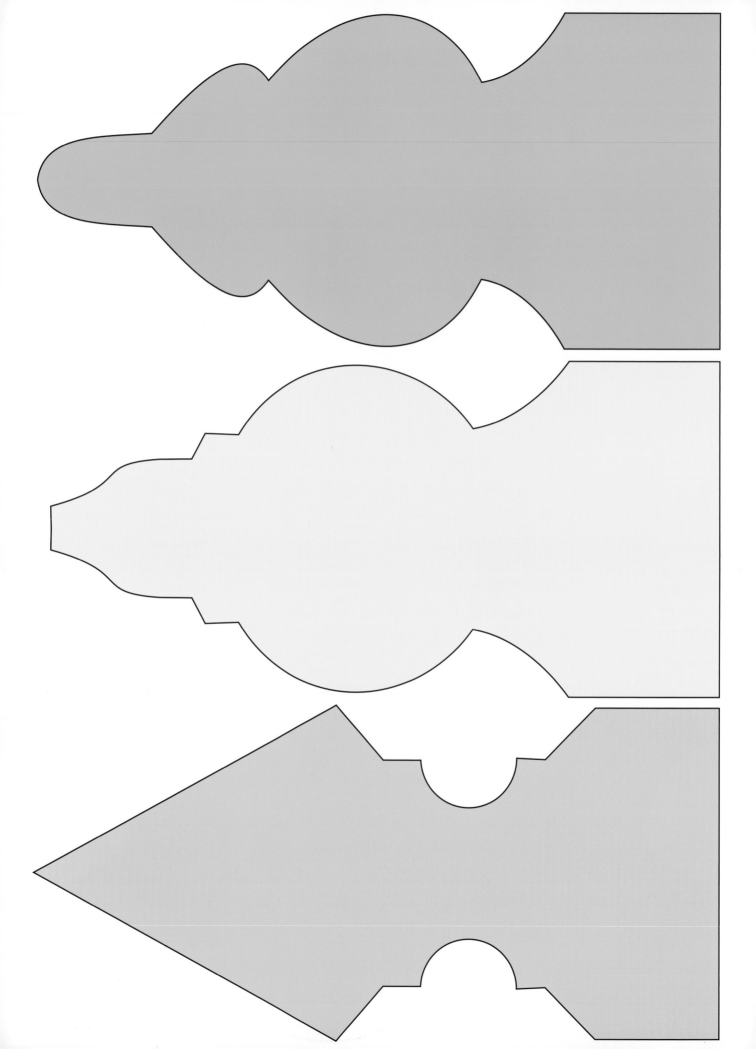

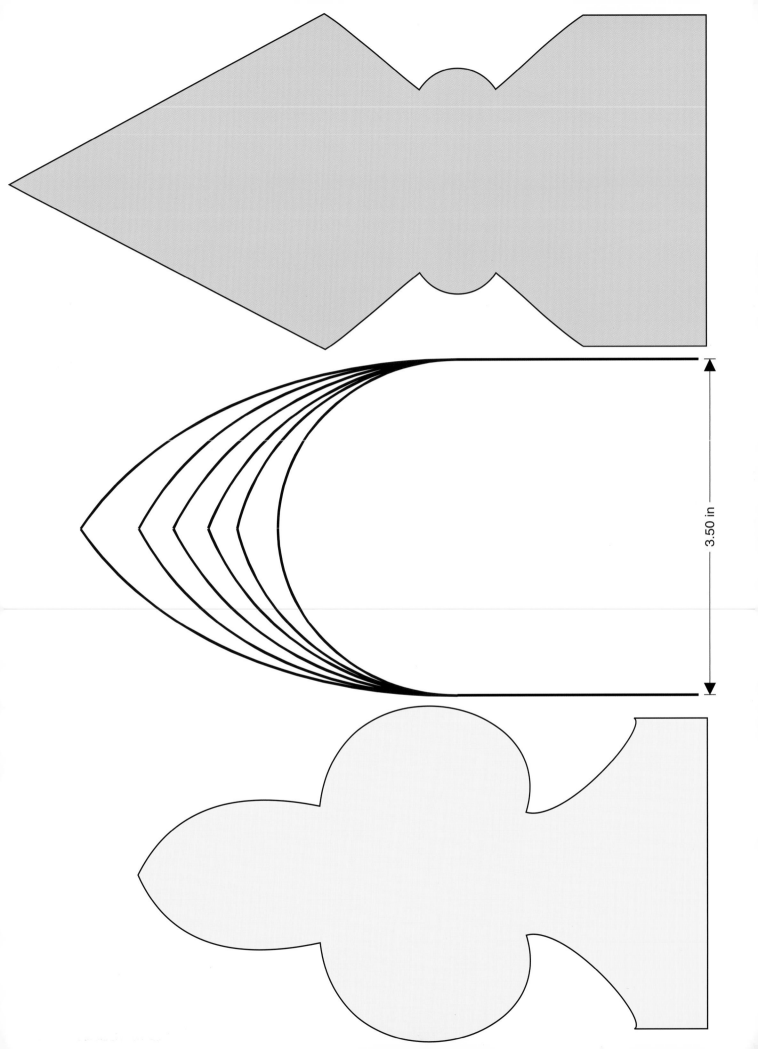

3.50 in

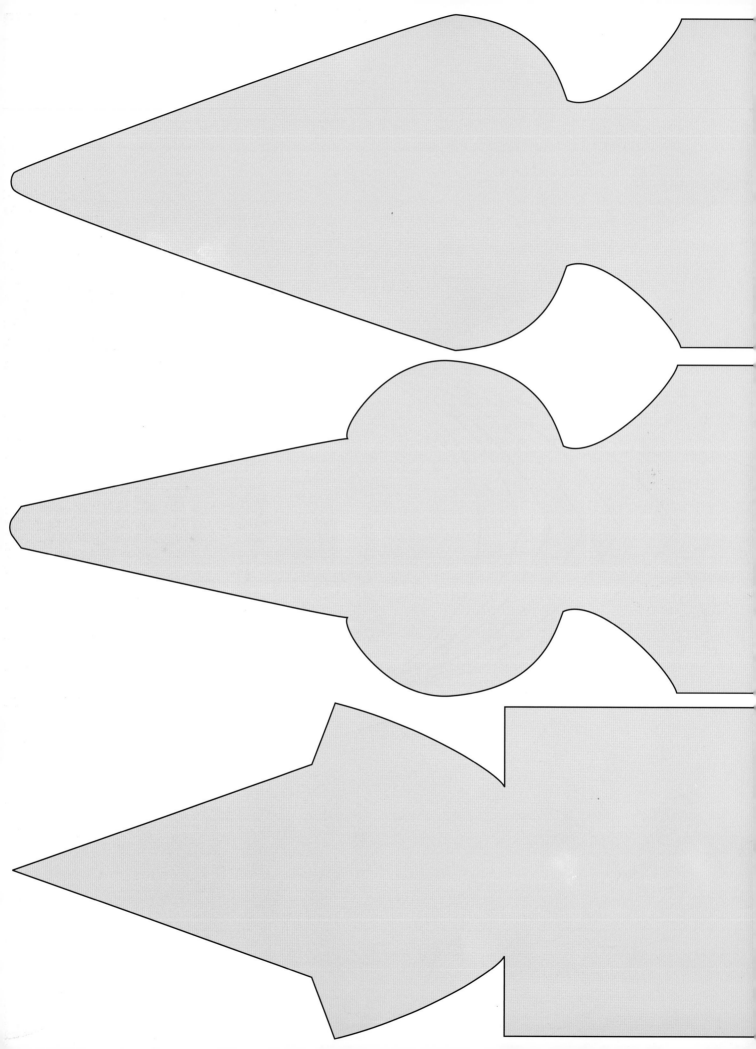

Cutouts for Closed-Spaced Pickets and Pickets and Separators

With close-spaced picket designs, and often with pickets and separator designs, cutouts are used to form windows between pickets and inside individual pickets. Rather than having an entire picket pattern with these window motifs, it is more versatile to have just the motif patterns themselves. This allows each fence maker to use the picket height and width of their choosing. Shorter picket fences will use fewer motifs per picket; taller ones can use more motifs.

It is a good idea to plan the motif layout on your fence. Your fence will look best if all the motifs are of the same general complexity and size. It is very difficult to do a random placing of motifs that looks attractive. It is also more time consuming; it means that many or all pickets will be different from each other. To help you understand how you can lay out these motifs, schematics of fences using these motifs are presented with the patterns.

In addition to the motif patterns in this book, there are many sources for others. Foam stamps and stencils from craft stores, old-fashioned cookie cutters, and clip art are all great sources for motifs for making window cutouts inside and between your pickets.

Whatever your passion, you can make a fun and whimsical fence using motifs that represent your interests.

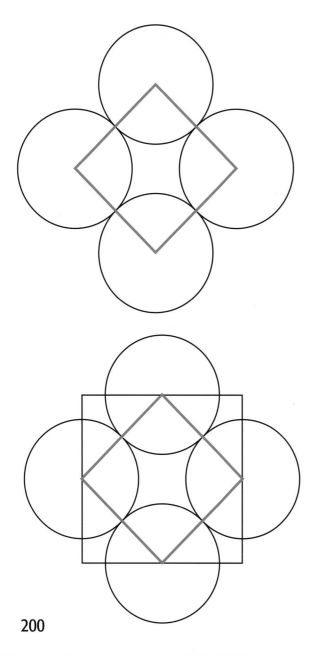

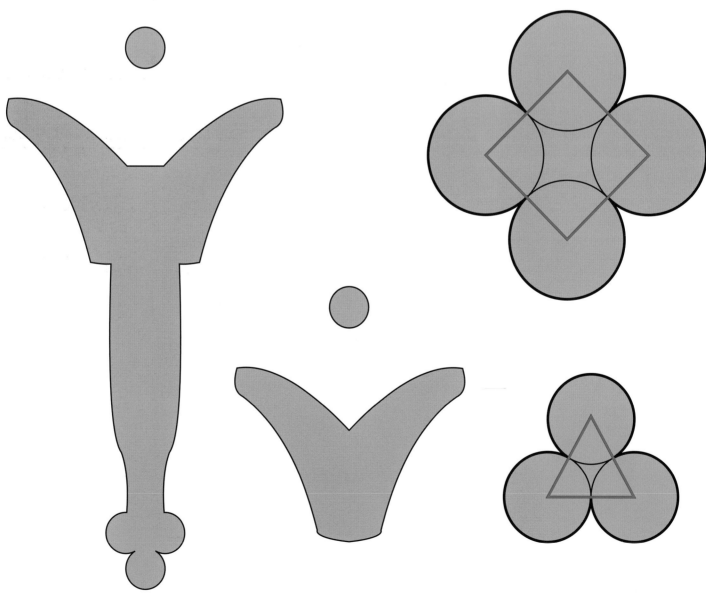

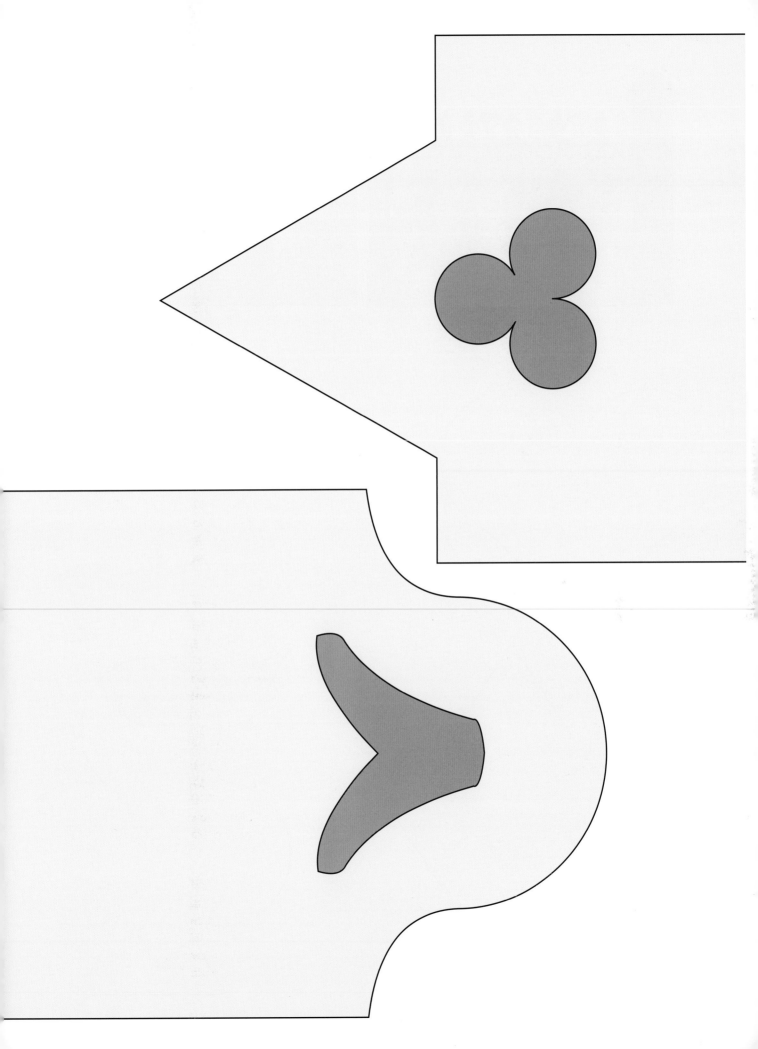

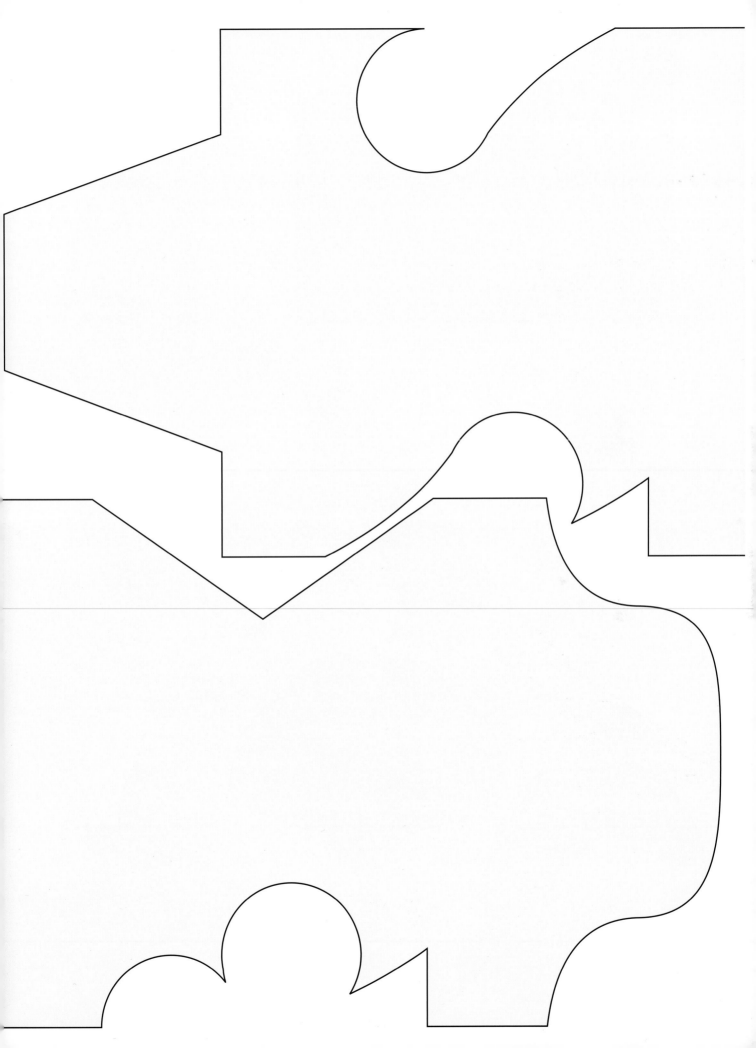

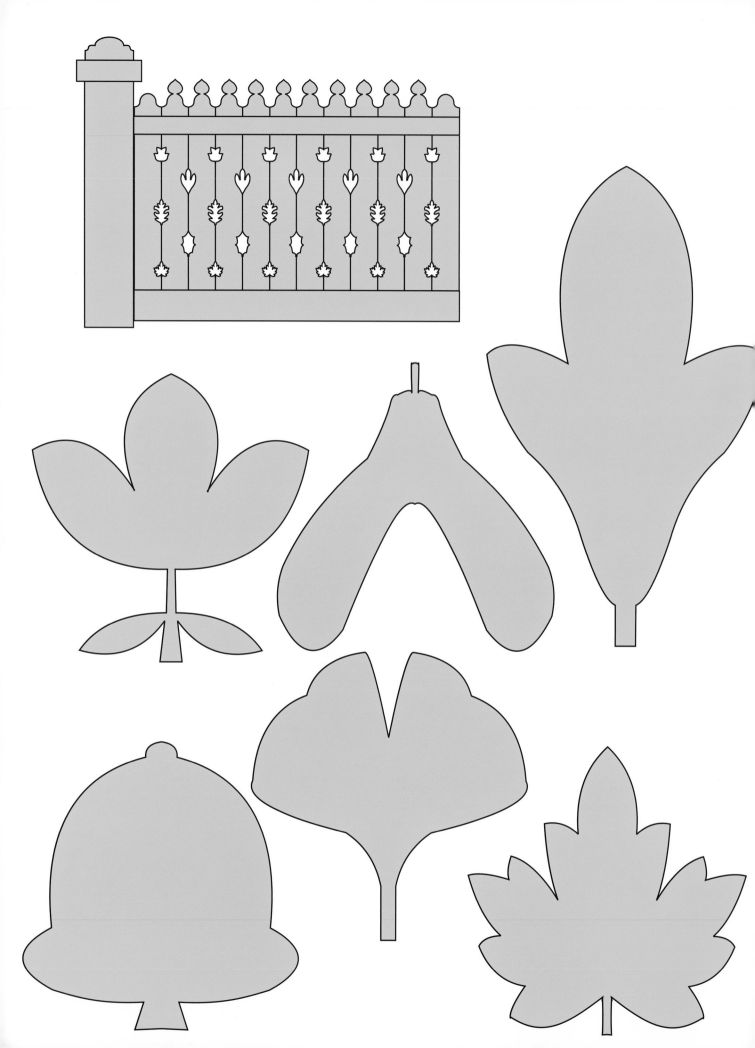

Square-Turned Finial Patterns

Finials made by square turning on the band saw.

When cutting finials, it is easier to cut the ones that maintain two areas of contact on the band saw table that are never cut. These finial patterns have an area near the base and farther up the body that will not be cut from the block of lumber. This means the lumber can always be rested flat on the table. Finials that do not maintain these uncut areas will be more difficult to cut out.

Finial patterns displayed with a vertical line beside them show the two areas that will remain uncut. See page 87 to see how to use a finial pattern to cut out a three-dimensional finial on the band saw using a square turning method.

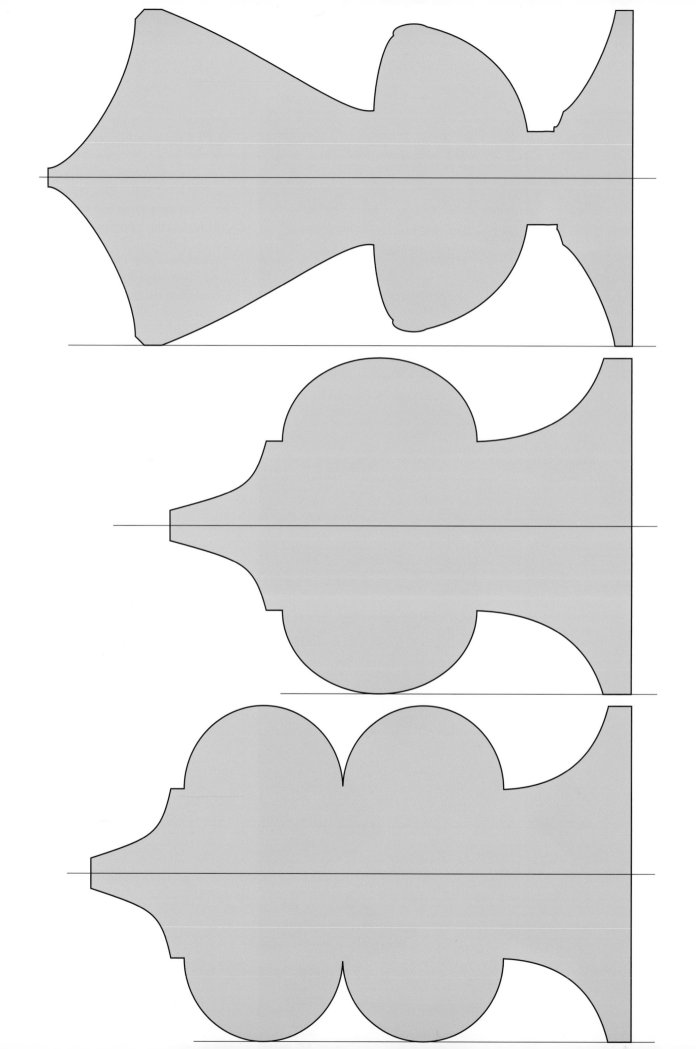

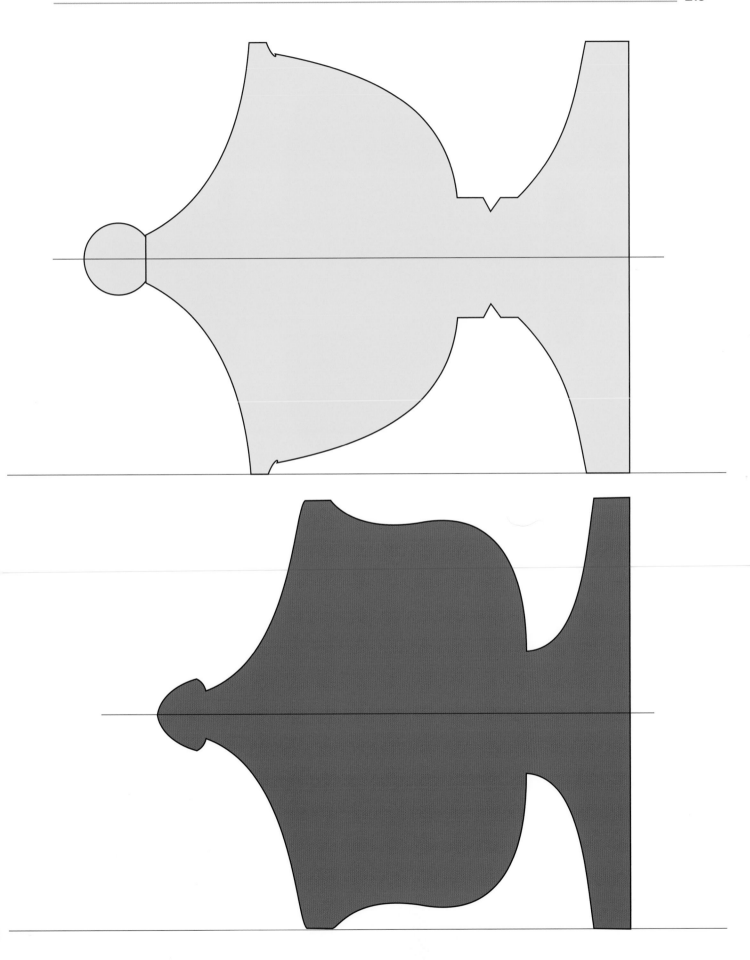

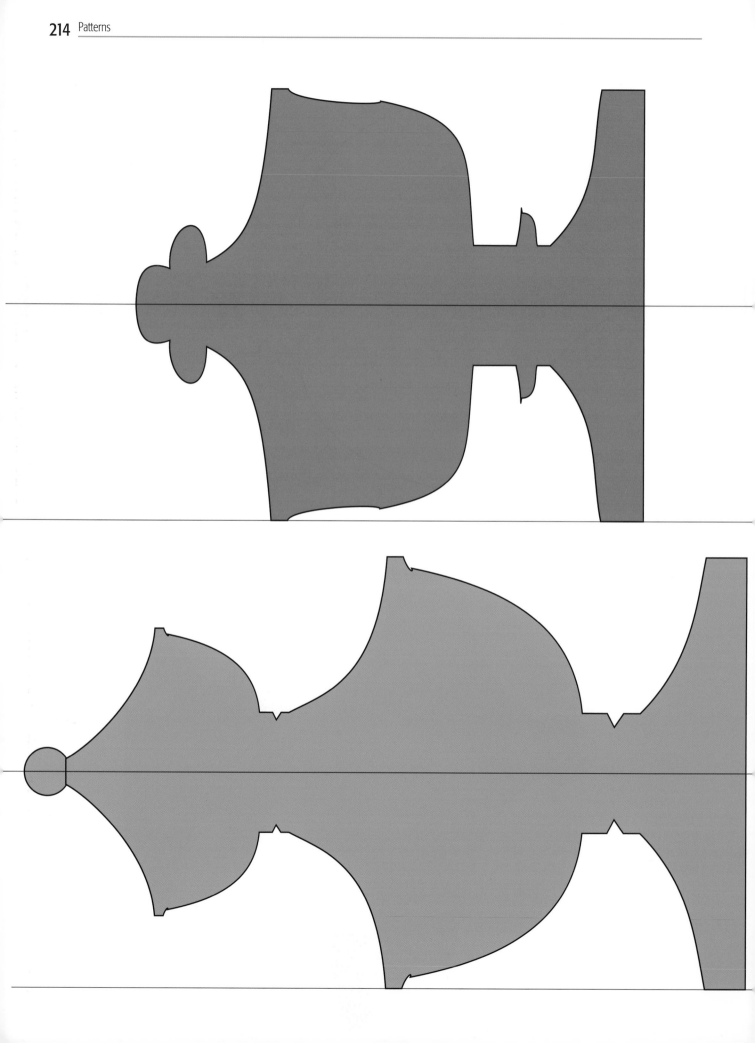

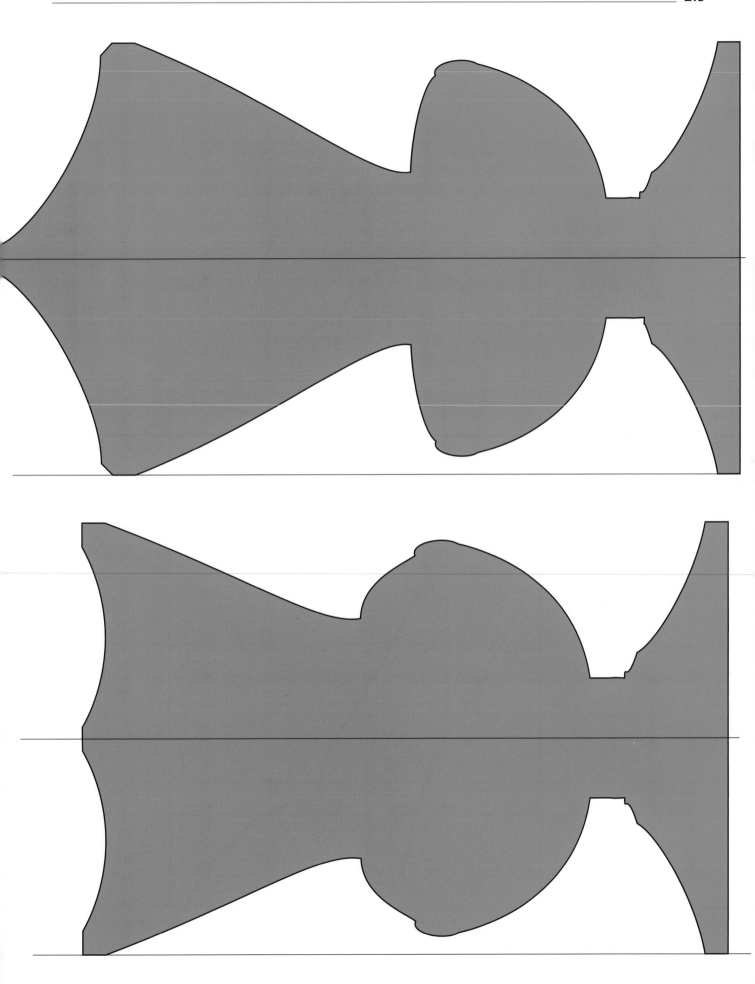

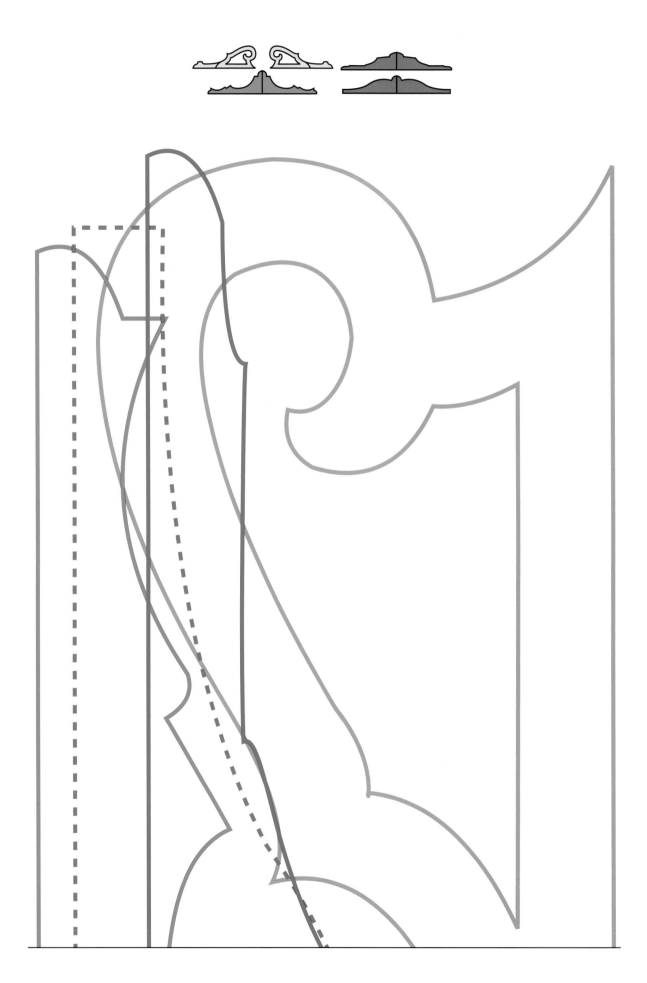

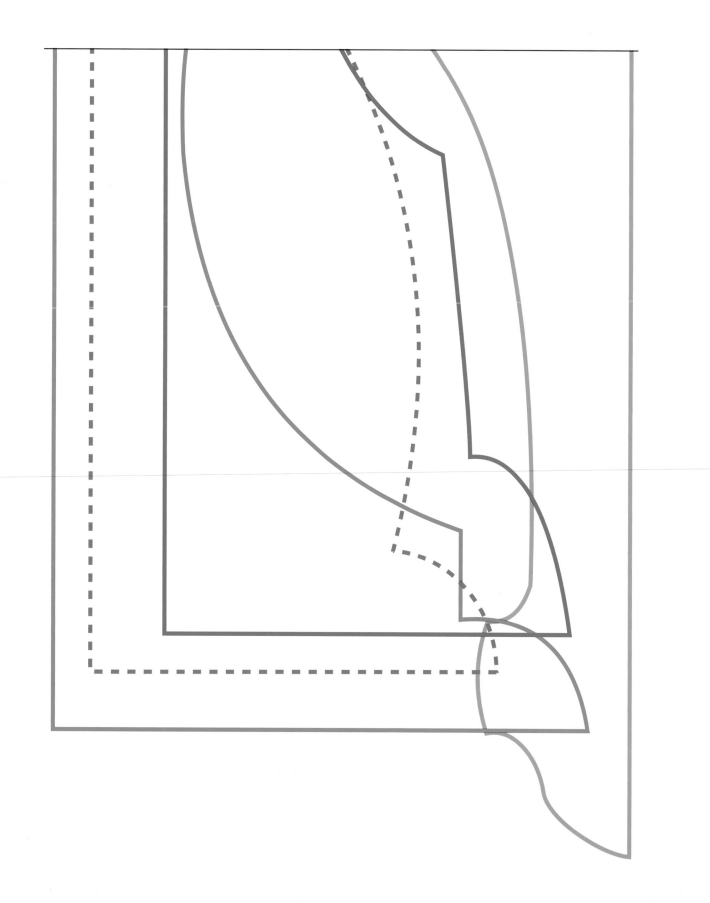

Sources

BJM Industries

12478 U.S. Route 422
Kittanning, PA 16201
(800) 683-3810
www.bjmindustries.com
Product: Millennium Plastic Lumber

Eco-Tech

6455 S. Pine Street
Burlington, WI 53105
(262) 539-3811
www.eco-tech.ws
Products: Eco-Tech Plastic Lumber,
Dura Max Structural Lumber

Fence America

198 Random Drive
New London, NC 28127
(800) 215-2740
woodshadesfencing.com
Product: WoodShades Composite Fencing

Fiberon

181 Random Drive
New London, NC 28127
(800) 573-8841
www.fiberondecking.com/products/fencing
Product: Fiberon Fencing

Grizzly Industrial

1821 Valencia St.
Bellingham, WA 98229
(800) 523-4777
www.grizzly.com
Products: Grizzly Tools